MURDER
BEYOND THE GRAVE

JAMES PATTERSON is one of the best-known and biggest-selling writers of all time. His books have sold in excess of 350 million copies worldwide. He is the author of some of the most popular series of the past two decades – the Alex Cross, Women's Murder Club, Detective Michael Bennett and Private novels – and he has written many other number one bestsellers including romance novels and stand-alone thrillers.

James is passionate about encouraging children to read. Inspired by his own son who was a reluctant reader, he also writes a range of books for young readers including the Middle School, I Funny, Treasure Hunters, House of Robots, Confessions and Maximum Ride series. James has donated millions in grants to independent bookshops and he has been the most borrowed author in UK libraries for the past ten years in a row. He lives in Florida with his wife and son.

Also by James Patterson

MURDER IS FOREVER TRUE CRIME

Murder, Interrupted
Home Sweet Murder

A list of more titles by James Patterson
is printed at the back of this book

JAMES PATTERSON
MURDER
BEYOND THE GRAVE

with Andrew Bourelle
and Christopher Charles

arrow books

3 5 7 9 10 8 6 4 2

Arrow Books
20 Vauxhall Bridge Road
London SW1V 2SA

Arrow Books is part of the Penguin Random House group of companies
whose addresses can be found at global.penguinrandomhouse.com

Penguin
Random House
UK

First published by Arrow Books in 2018

www.penguin.co.uk

A CIP catalogue record for this book is available from the British Library.

ISBN 9781787460812

Printed and bound by Clays Ltd, St Ives Plc

Penguin Random House is committed to a sustainable future for our
business, our readers and our planet. This book is made from Forest
Stewardship Council® certified paper.

Dear Reader,

Above all else I'm a storyteller. I craft stories for insatiable readers. And though my books may seem over-the-top to some, I find that I am most often inspired by real life. After all, truth is stranger than fiction.

The crimes in this book are 100% real. Certain elements of the stories, some scenes and dialogue, locations, names, and characters have been fictionalized, but these stories are about real people committing real crimes, with real, horrifying consequences.

And as terrifying and visceral as it is to read about these crimes gone wrong, there's something to remember: the bad guy always gets caught.

If you can't get enough of these true crimes, please watch the pulse-racing new television series Murder Is Forever, where you'll see these shocking crimes come to life.

I hope you're as haunted by these accounts as I am. They'll remind you that though humans have the capacity for incredible kindness, we also have the capacity for unspeakable violence and depravity.

CONTENTS

MURDER BEYOND THE GRAVE

James Patterson with Andrew Bourelle   1

MURDER IN PARADISE

James Patterson with Christopher Charles   129

MURDER BEYOND THE GRAVE

CHAPTER 1

THE MAN GASPS FOR air and claws at the plywood siding of his prison. He's inside a coffin that is six feet long and three feet wide.

Rivulets of sweat pour from his brow. His shirt is soaked. His heart is thumping like he's just run up a flight of stairs. His skull is throbbing with a nauseating headache.

He has been buried alive.

At gunpoint.

A stranger, disguised with a ski mask and motorcycle helmet, had kidnapped him, had clipped handcuffs around his wrists, and later, when he forced him into the box, he cut the chain between the cuffs but left the circles of metal clasped tightly to his wrists.

The kidnapper left three items in the coffin: a gallon jug of cloudy water, a pile of candy bars, and a car battery attached to a caged lightbulb. He has gulped half the water already but hasn't touched the candy bars. He isn't sure how long he's been in here. The lightbulb is starting to dim.

He looks up at a small piece of PVC pipe sticking through the plywood, and he puts his mouth over the tube, trying to draw big gulps of fresh air. But though he's in good shape, his lungs strain. No matter how much air he pulls in, his chest is still heaving, still gasping for more.

He knows what's happening. He's running out of oxygen. The pipe isn't doing enough to circulate fresh air into the chamber.

He pushes up against the plywood and pounds on the wood with his fists.

"Help!" he screams.

But his vocal cords are raw from yelling so much. And he can barely catch his breath as it is.

He tries to calm his panicked breathing, taking long, slow breaths. His head is pounding.

Keep it together, he tells himself. *Calm down!*

He remembered what the masked man said when he put him in here, that this is all about money.

Everything's going to be fine. I've worked out all the details. You're not going to die.

But he is beginning to think his kidnapper is never coming back.

The air smells of sour sweat, plywood, and caulk. And hidden behind those odors, barely noticeable, is the smell of freshly dug soil—the smell of his grave.

He presses his trembling hands against the plywood again. This time, when he pushes upward, straining with all his strength, he feels some give in the earth. He feels a moment of hope. But when he releases the pressure, the board sags inward, like a mineshaft nearing its inevitable collapse.

The light flickers. He takes deep breaths. Long inhalations. Slow exhalations. He tries to calm his nerves.

He closes his eyes and, as he waits for the light to die and the darkness to envelop him, he thinks of the faces of his children and the woman he loves. He hopes they know how much he loves them.

CHAPTER 2

January 1987
Eight months earlier

DANNY EDWARDS WALKS DOWN a sidewalk in Chicago, his head down, his fists buried in his coat. Flakes of snow drift in the air. Danny's breath comes out in bursts of visible vapor. Cars drive by, slicing through gray slush.

Danny is thirty years old, well dressed, and handsome. Under ordinary circumstances, he would seem like a friendly guy, but today he has a determined look on his face. He's anxious.

He pushes through the door into a steak house and is greeted by a rush of warm air, a cloud of cigarette smoke, and a barrel-chested host who lights up when he sees him.

"Yo, Danny," the man says, his Chicago accent thick. "Long time no see, eh?"

When the man opens his arms to give Danny a hug, Danny awkwardly thrusts a hand out for a shake instead.

"How've you been?" Danny says, feigning a smile.

"Oh, you know," says his longtime associate, who,

unfazed by the rebuffed embrace, claps Danny on the shoulder. "Same ol', same ol'."

Danny opens his mouth for more small talk, but the host cuts him off with a nod toward the kitchen.

"He's waiting for you in the back. Told me to send you in straightaway."

Danny makes his way toward the rear of the restaurant, walking through tendrils of cigarette smoke. The room is full of low-hanging lamps and checkerboard tablecloths. He enters a redbrick hallway and walks past the kitchen, where white-clad cooks shout over a flaming grill, and then past the dish room, where a kid with pimples on his face and a cigarette between his lips is blasting dirty plates with a high-powered spray nozzle.

In the very back of the restaurant is an oak door, standing ajar, and Danny knocks gently and pokes his head inside.

"Hey, Mitch," Danny says, trying to sound nonchalant.

"Sit down," Mitch says to Danny without any of the good cheer the host displayed when Danny entered the restaurant.

Danny sits in a leather chair across from Mitch, who is leaning over a white platter. There are no vegetables on the plate, no sides whatsoever. Just a sixteen-ounce porterhouse barely seared on the outside and as bloody as a bullet wound on the inside.

Mitch, an intimidating sixtysomething man with silver-streaked hair and cold, dark eyes, saws into the meat and pops a dripping bite into his mouth.

"How's it going?" Danny says.

"Cut the crap," Mitch says, his voice like a garbage disposal filled with broken glass. "Where's my money?"

Danny's façade breaks. He nervously glances around the room. "Here's the thing, Mitch," he says, and then hesitates to continue.

Mitch stares at him. He holds his fork in one hand and a steak knife in the other, but his meal is forgotten. His attention is focused on Danny.

Danny takes a deep breath and then rips the Band-Aid off.

"The cops nabbed my cocaine," Danny says. "The whole supply."

Mitch's expression is unreadable.

"I'm lucky they didn't get *me*," Danny says.

Mitch continues to stare, saying nothing. Danny fidgets in his chair.

"Listen," Danny says. "I've got it all worked out. My buyers are still interested. They're hungry for product. I just need another kilo. I'll give all the profits to you. It will cover what I owe you *and* the new bag. You know I'm good for it."

Mitch returns to his steak without speaking. Danny waits. He can't sit still. He pulls at the collar of his shirt and wipes a bead of sweat from his brow. Mitch takes his time cutting off another bloody hunk of steak.

"So you're going to pay me double?" Mitch says, without looking at Danny.

"Of course."

"And a penalty fee?"

Danny hesitates. "If that's what it takes. I want to make things right."

"What's up with you?" Mitch says, raising his eyes and fixing them on Danny. "You seem a little bit off. Why are you sweating so much?"

CHAPTER 3

OUTSIDE IN A NONDESCRIPT panel van, two police officers listen with headphones.

"Damn it," says the first officer. "He's been made."

"Wait," says the other. "This guy Danny is a slick operator. Let's see what he does."

High-tech equipment lines one side of the van's interior, and the first officer adjusts a knob to try to hear the conversation better.

"*I seem a bit off?*" Danny asks.

"*Yeah,*" Mitch says, his gravelly voice particularly jumbled in the earphones. "*Jumpy.*"

"*Jumpy?*"

"*Yeah,*" Mitch says, getting frustrated now. "*You gonna repeat everything I say?*"

"*Sorry,*" Danny says.

"*What I'm wondering is if the cops nabbed the cocaine you were selling, how is it that they didn't nab you?*"

The two cops look at each other.

"Get ready to call in the team," the first one says. "I don't want a dead informant on our hands."

The detectives spent weeks putting this operation together. After they busted Danny Edwards, they convinced him that they wouldn't charge him if he wore a wire and helped them bring down his supplier.

Danny Edwards is a little fish—they want the Big Kahuna.

The plan is simple: once Mitch shows Danny the drugs, Danny is supposed to say a code phrase. Then the police will come rushing in. The only other reason they would come rushing in would be if Danny seemed to be in danger. Danny's a low-level hoodlum, but they don't want his blood on their hands.

"I'm making the call," the first officer says, picking up a walkie-talkie.

"Wait!" the second says, and they both go quiet as they listen.

"How is it that they didn't nab me?" Danny whispers.

"I swear to God you better stop repeating everything I say."

"Okay, okay," Danny says. *"Here's what happened."*

Danny explains how he's been keeping his supply of drugs at a construction site down the road from where he does most of his deals, not in his own home. The house is a skeleton of two-by-fours and plywood flooring. Just now, the roof is getting shingled and the walls are being covered in drywall. But the central air ducts are installed, and it's a convenient place to keep a brick of coke hidden and dry.

"That part of the house has already been inspected, you see. No one looks in there."

"Why don't you just keep your coke at your own house like a normal drug dealer?" Mitch asks.

"Are you kidding?" Danny says. *"My girlfriend would have a fit. I'd be sleeping on the street if she found out there were any drugs in the house."*

Danny goes on to explain that he was selling to a couple guys he hadn't seen before. They were asking for more than he had on him. He should have known better, he admits, but he told them to wait and he'd be back in thirty minutes. He walked to the construction site without realizing he was being followed. Once he'd reached into the vent and pulled out the brick, two other guys came running from the corner of the house waving guns and badges.

Danny took off on foot and lost them when he hid in the rafters of another half-finished house at the construction site.

"I saw them grab the coke," Danny says, *"and then I snuck off."*

"And these cops don't know who you are?" Mitch asks.

"No way, man. That's why I walked to the construction site. They don't have my plate number. They don't know the car I drive. They saw my face, but I never ended up selling them anything. Even if they found out who I was, they couldn't do anything. They've got nothing."

The two police officers listen as the conversation in their headphones goes quiet for a moment.

"You were right," says the first officer.

"Told you he was a slick operator."

"That was such a convincing story he almost fooled *me*," says the first cop.

"*If I give you more*," they hear Mitch say, "*are you going to be careful?*"

"*Thank you so much*," Danny says. "*I'm so happy I could kiss a pig.*"

"Did you hear that?" says the first police officer.

The other officer nods and barks into his walkie-talkie, "Move! Move! Move! The drug deal is going down!"

CHAPTER 4

"DON'T GO KISSING ANY pigs just yet," Mitch growls at Danny. "You're still in hot water."

Danny dabs more sweat from his forehead.

"This is your last chance." Mitch points his knife toward Danny. "You know what happens if you mess this up?"

A drop of red juice drips off the blade of the knife.

Danny opens his mouth to answer, but then they hear a commotion going on outside the office door. There's yelling, then the sound of pans clattering and glass breaking. Then comes an earsplitting crash, as if someone dropped a whole tray of dinner plates outside the office door.

"What in the holy hell is going on out there?" Mitch snarls.

Mitch stands to his feet just as the door bursts open, crashing against the wall with a bang. In seconds, the office is full of police officers pointing shotguns and pistols at Mitch and Danny.

"Hands up!" a cop yells.

Danny obliges. Mitch ignores the request.

"What's going on here?" he barks. "What do you think you're doing?"

"You two are under arrest," one cop says, leveling a pistol at Mitch's forehead.

Another cop grabs Mitch and shoves him against his desk. He kicks Mitch's legs into a wide stance and begins patting him down. Another officer shoves Danny against the wall and begins patting him down as well.

"Where are the drugs?" one of the officers asks Mitch.

"What drugs?" Mitch says. "This is a family restaurant. It's a law-abiding business."

The cop gets close to Mitch's ear and says, "You're the biggest drug dealer in the city. You know it. We know it. Everybody knows it. And now you're finally going down for it."

"Where's your evidence?"

The cops glance around the room, as if they're expecting to see a brick of coke sitting out in the open. There isn't anything but Mitch's half-eaten steak.

"Don't worry," the cop says, pulling Mitch's hands behind his back and cuffing them. "We'll find the evidence, even if we have to tear this place apart."

A cop yanks one of Danny's arms behind his back, fastens a cuff around it, and then pulls his other arm back and locks them together.

"Ouch," Danny mumbles.

"What's wrong?" a cop says. "Don't like being locked

up? Get used to it. We're going to lock you up until you're old enough to collect social security."

The police begin searching the office, flinging open drawers on the desk and turning over furniture. Danny watches them search, then raises his eyes to look at Mitch.

Mitch is glaring at him, his eyes focused and murderous.

A cold chill slithers up Danny's spine. Mitch doesn't say a word, but his expression tells Danny everything he needs to know.

Mitch's expression says, *I know it was you.*

CHAPTER 5

DANNY SITS IN THE rear of an unmarked police car as it rolls past the welcome sign for the city of Kankakee, Illinois. In the front seats sit the same officers who were in the panel van earlier, his handlers for the undercover operation. They are detectives with KAMEG—the Kankakee Area Metropolitan Drug Enforcement Group. Danny has forgotten their names. Both were friendly to him before, but now things are different. Ever since the bust went awry, they've been alternating between cold indifference and fiery antagonism.

"You know you could have taken these damn handcuffs off me," Danny says, shifting his body to find a comfortable way to sit in the seat while his hands are still locked behind his back.

The officer in the passenger seat—a fortysomething man with blond hair, sideburns, and a mustache—shifts around to look at Danny. His eyes glare at Danny with nearly the same rage that had been burning in Mitch's eyes.

"You're lucky we're not throwing your ass in jail," the officer says.

"Hey," Danny says, shrugging his shoulders, "I did my part."

"You were supposed to say the code phrase *after* you saw the coke. Not before."

"He was about to pull it out," Danny says. "I was sure of it."

"It's our fault," says the driver, a man about Danny's age with a buzz cut that makes him look as if he just got out of the marines. "We assumed this high school dropout knew the difference between *before* and *after*."

"My three-year-old knows the difference between before and after," says the officer with the mustache.

"Yeah, but your son's human." The driver looks in the rearview mirror and fixes his eyes on Danny. "Not a rat."

"Very funny," Danny says. "You weren't calling me a rat when I agreed to help you."

"That was back when we thought you were actually going to help us," the cop says. "Not screw us over."

"If it was up to me," the mustached officer says, "I'd put your lying ass in jail. You reneged on your agreement as far as I'm concerned."

"Well, it's not up to you," Danny says, unable to hide a smile. "The state's attorney says I fulfilled the terms of my deal."

The cop in the passenger seat looks over at the driver. "I told you he was a slick operator."

The driver says nothing, and quiet overtakes the car.

Danny looks out the window. The car crosses a bridge over the Kankakee River. Its water is gray in the January light, and the trees lining the banks are leafless and lean.

Soon they're driving through downtown Kankakee, a short strip of old brick storefronts. With a population of about twenty-five thousand people, Kankakee is a nice little town—quaint, quiet, and close enough to Chicago that residents can get their big-city fix whenever they need to.

Danny watches the storefronts roll by, remembering growing up here. He'd ridden his bike into town on summer afternoons. He'd gone swimming in the river. He'd snuck into train cars at the old depot and smoked marijuana with his friends.

His parents were well off, and he'd never been left wanting. As an adult, he'd done well for himself—just not by obeying the law. Up until recently, he'd been making four thousand dollars a week selling cocaine. He'd owned a riverfront house in an upscale neighborhood, and he'd also been making enough to lease a split-level town house for his girlfriend, Nancy. He paid for her place because he didn't want her and her eight-year-old son, Benji, to be close to his drug-dealing operations.

Life had been great. He'd been planning to buy a boat.

But then KAMEG agents raided his Aroma Park home, seizing ten thousand dollars in cash and two hundred grams of cocaine—with a street value of twenty thousand. The story of the narrow escape that he told to Mitch was a complete fabrication. The truth is he'd been busted red-handed.

A month ago, he'd had the world at his feet. Now he's sleeping in Nancy's town house, trying to figure out how to make the monthly payment. All the money he had in the world is gone. Life as he once knew it is now over.

"Why are you looking so gloomy?" the officer in the passenger seat says to him. "You just lucked into a get-out-of-jail-free card."

"It doesn't feel that way," Danny says. "What am I supposed to do now?"

As the police car rolls up in front of Nancy's town house, the two officers look at each other, incredulous. The driver turns around and glares at Danny.

"Why don't you try getting a job like everybody else."

CHAPTER 6

August 1987

DANNY SWINGS HIS HAMMER and drives a framing nail into a two-by-four. He stands inside the skeleton of a house under construction, sweating in the summer humidity. He reaches into his tool belt, pulls out another nail, and lines it up. He takes a swing and misses the nail—hitting his thumb instead.

"Damn it!" he shouts, throwing his hammer down onto the plywood floor.

He shakes his hand, trying to wring out the pain. He checks his watch. It's not quite quitting time, but close enough.

He collects his hammer and heads over to the foreman, who hands him a check. Danny stares in disbelief at the numbers on the paystub.

"Uncle Sam sure takes a bite, don't he?" the foreman says.

And people say I'm a crook, Danny thinks.

He almost opens his mouth to ask for more hours. He

sure could use the money. But he hates the work. There's got to be an easier way to make money.

He climbs into his van and heads home. At a stoplight, he examines the palms of his hands. The soft flesh is full of blisters. He keeps waiting for calluses to form and for his skin to toughen up, but it hasn't happened yet.

I'm not cut out for this type of work, he thinks.

The only problem is that the one type of work he is cut out for is illegal. He's been walking the straight and narrow since January because he knows that another bust will put him in prison for who knows how long. There will be no leniency this time. No deal.

No get-out-of-jail-free card.

He pulls up in front of the town house, which is in need of a new paint job.

Inside, he finds Nancy crouched in the kitchen behind the dishwasher, which she's slid out from the counter. A slick of soapy water covers the linoleum floor. Her son, Benji—oblivious to the difficulties of the world—is playing in the puddle. Nancy has a roll of duct tape and is wrapping it around a pipe.

"What the hell are you doing?" Danny says.

"The damn thing's leaking again," Nancy says without looking up.

Nancy Rish is a knockout. Twenty-five years old. Petite. Platinum blond. When she dresses up for a night on the town, she looks like a Barbie doll.

But right now, her hair is damp and hanging in her eyes, her sweatpants are soaked with soapy water, and she has grease on her hands and forearms like she's an auto-shop mechanic instead of a stay-at-home mom.

"That should do it," she says, and stands up.

She presses the button to start the dishwasher again. The motor begins to hum, and they watch for more water leaking out. It appears she fixed whatever was wrong.

She grabs a mop and starts to clean up the floor. Danny knows he should help, but he's dog tired after working all day, so he just watches her.

When she's finished mopping, she leans against the handle and says, "You know, I've been thinking. It's time I go back to work."

"No," Danny says without considering it.

"Honey," she says. "We need the money."

Benji is walking around the kitchen, searching for puddles. There's no more water for him to splash in, but his shoes are wet and he keeps leaving dirty footprints on the linoleum.

"I'll think of something," Danny says. "I'll get back on my feet. I promise."

Nancy approaches him, and even in her soaked sweatpants and dirty tank top, she is still beautiful. She puts her arms around his neck and pulls his face down for a long kiss.

"I'm so proud of you for not dealing anymore," she says. "Times are tough right now, but they're going to get better. You're doing the right thing. Let me help you."

Danny shakes his head. When he first met her, Nancy had been working two jobs and somehow taking care of Benji in what little free time she had. She'd gotten pregnant and married as a teenager and ever since she divorced her husband, she'd worked odd jobs: waitressing, selling makeup, cleaning houses. He'd been able to take her from that life. He'd be damned if he was the reason she had to go back to it.

He wraps his arms around her and embraces her. She closes her eyes and rests her head on his chest.

They hear Benji splashing in a puddle.

"I thought I got it all," Nancy says, opening her eyes.

The dishwasher is leaking again.

CHAPTER 7

DANNY DRIVES DOWN THE tree-lined streets of the tony neighborhood where his parents live. His van's window is down because even though it's only midmorning, the day is hot and humid.

Danny parks his van in front of his parents' home, a big two-story house with a large front porch with columns flanking the front door. He cuts through the grass and takes the porch steps two at a time.

He raps on the door and waits. He can hear a lawn mower down the street and somewhere kids are playing and laughing. He feels a pang of nostalgia for his own childhood, a time when life was simpler and easier.

When his father comes to the door, Danny expects to be invited in, but instead George Edwards steps out onto the porch and closes the door behind him. His hair is grayer than the last time Danny saw him. His eyes look weary.

"What do you want, Danny?"

Danny frowns. "How about a 'Hello, son, it's good to see you'?"

His father crosses his arms and leans against the porch railing. He repeats his question. "What do you want, Danny?"

Danny huffs. "It's nice to see you too," he says sarcastically.

When his dad doesn't say anything else, Danny says, "Look, Dad, I need a loan. I just need some help getting on my feet. I promise I will pay you back."

"No."

"I've cleaned up my act," Danny says. "I'm staying out of trouble, making important changes in my life. Nancy and I need a little help, that's all."

"No," his father says. "I'm done helping you."

Danny opens his mouth to object, but his father doesn't give him the chance.

"I offered you a place in the family business," his father says. "But you didn't want to be an electrician. Then I offered you a job at the grocery store I own. You didn't want anything to do with that either."

Danny doesn't have a defense. He's always preferred easy money to hard work and started selling marijuana in high school.

"May I also remind you," his father says, "that when you dropped out of high school and married Peggy, I gave you a house—a *house*, Danny!"

Danny lowers his head. After he divorced his wife so he could be with Nancy, he and his ex-wife had sold the house, and he'd used his share to get in the door of the cocaine business.

"Look," Danny says, trying to sound sincere, "I understand why you don't want to help me. I've screwed up in the past. But I'm really trying to do the right thing here."

His father takes a deep breath, and Danny feels relieved that he's finally gotten to the old man.

"I hope that what you say is true, Danny. I hope you've cleaned up your act. But I won't help you anymore."

Danny's hope evaporates.

"You've hurt me too many times in the past," his dad says.

With that, his father opens the front door and walks back inside. Danny can hear the click as his father throws the dead bolt.

"Well, to hell with you," Danny mutters, "you old son of a bitch."

He climbs back into his van and begins driving through Kankakee. He isn't ready to go home and face Nancy. He knows the city well, and he guides the van through the nicest neighborhoods. He looks at the big houses, with vast green front yards and shiny sports cars parked in the driveways.

His parents were never millionaires, but they were well off. He was born with a silver spoon in his mouth. He wishes now he could reverse the decisions that led him to where he is today. If he had finished high school, he could have gotten his electrician's union card. He could be running the business with his older brothers. Or the grocery store—he could be managing it now.

But selling drugs was too easy.

He passes a particularly opulent house with an expansive front yard and a wraparound front porch. There is a red Ferrari parked in the driveway in front of a detached garage. Three barefoot boys are running through a sprinkler, a teenager and two younger boys who look like twins.

A man wearing glasses, a polo shirt, and a pair of khaki shorts steps out on the front porch. The guy has a smile on his face like he has it all.

"I wish I had that guy's life," Danny says to himself, and he drives on.

CHAPTER 8

STEPHEN SMALL DOESN'T EVEN notice the white panel van driving past his house, let alone the scraggly haired man behind the wheel who is leering covetously at his home. He only pays attention to his boys, who are taking turns running through the sprinkler.

His twins, Barrett and Christopher, are laughing as they dart through the water. His older son, Ramsey, tries to do a cartwheel over the spray, but slips and falls into the grass, howling with laughter.

Stephen chuckles to himself and heads toward the Ferrari parked in the driveway.

"Oh, Stephen," his wife, Nancy, calls from behind him.

Stephen turns to see his wife holding up a set of keys.

"Forget something?" she asks.

Stephen laughs and heads back toward the porch. His

wife of eighteen years has a bright friendly smile that he fell in love with early in their courtship.

"Thanks, hon," Stephen says, giving her a hug and a kiss on the cheek.

"Where are you going, Dad?" Ramsey calls out to him.

"I've got to go to the boat shop and pick up a few things," he says.

"Then can we go out on the river?"

"You bet," Stephen says.

He fires up the Ferrari and pulls out of the driveway. The two-hundred-thousand-dollar car has a V8 engine, but Stephen doesn't push the car too fast, especially in residential areas. He is a careful driver.

He takes a slight detour on his way into town and cruises down Kankakee's Riverview Historic District. He slows and creeps past a large, unusual-looking house on a spacious lot. There are a handful of workers going into and out of the building.

The twelve-thousand-square-foot house is a historic fixture in the community. Built in 1901, the house was designed by famed architect Frank Lloyd Wright. It has twelve bedrooms and more than a hundred windows.

Just this month the house was placed on the National Register of Historic Places. In Stephen Small's view, the house is the jewel of the Riverview Historic District.

But Stephen isn't just another sightseer slowing down to admire the house.

He owns it.

A year ago, he bought the house with the intention of

renovating it and perhaps one day turning it into a bed-and-breakfast. The B. Harley Bradley House, named for the original owner, is Stephen's passion project.

He doesn't stop the Ferrari, just slows down, checks to make sure the house is okay, and then speeds along toward his destination.

He has faith in the workers, but he can't help himself. Stephen keeps an eye on the house whenever he's in the area.

If anything happened to the house, he isn't sure what he would do.

CHAPTER 9

DANNY PULLS HIS VAN into a parking space at the local boat shop and strolls in through the door. The air-conditioning feels refreshing on his clammy skin.

"Hey there," the manager says. "What can I do you for?"

Danny explains that he needs his deposit back on a boat he put a down payment on.

"I don't have the riverfront property I did when I planned to buy the boat," Danny explains.

After his arrest, Danny moved out of the river house he had used as the base of operations for his drug deals. Not only could he not afford it anymore, but he was also afraid that Mitch would find him there and exact revenge for Danny leading police to his restaurant. He hoped Mitch wouldn't hold a grudge since he'd led the police astray. He'd known Mitch didn't keep any drugs in the restaurant, but he wasn't sure Mitch would see what he'd done as a favor.

"You want your deposit back?" the manager asks. "You

know you don't get all your money back, just a portion. It says so in the agreement you signed."

Danny scratches his head and reluctantly says that he understands.

"I need the money," Danny says. "There's no way I can buy a boat any time soon."

The manager walks into a back office to collect the paperwork and write Danny a check, and Danny stands and waits, looking around. He studies the selection of skis, life jackets, and boat-maintenance tools. He feels a wave of depression come over him. There is such a difference between the life he lives now and the life he had a year ago—the life he thought he would continue to have forever.

As if he needs another reminder of the difference between what he has and what he wants, Danny watches as a red Ferrari zips into the parking lot and parks next to his van. The two vehicles couldn't look more different. His van is dingy and dented, with rust growing on the doors and a filthy film on the windshield. The Ferrari is gleaming and red, as if its owner washes and waxes it every time he takes it out for a spin.

When the driver steps out, Danny can't believe it—it's the same man he'd seen on the drive here. The preppy man with glasses at the house where the kids were playing in the sprinkler.

The man walks in the door and starts down the aisle, whistling without a care in the world. Danny stares at him.

When the man comes to the counter with a few bottles

of cleaning products and a package of sponges, he nods at Danny and says, "Afternoon."

The manager comes back to the counter and tells Danny that he'll ring the customer up quickly and then take care of Danny's refund.

"Getting your boat cleaned up?" the manager says politely.

"Yes, sir," the man says enthusiastically. "Gonna take my boys out tubing this afternoon."

The man says he has a thirty-foot, five-hundred-horsepower speedboat.

"The kids love it," he says, taking his receipt and heading out the door.

Danny and the manager both watch as the Ferrari glides out of the parking lot.

"I wish I had that kind of money," Danny says.

"You and me both," the clerk says, handing Danny a check. "Do you know who that is?"

Danny shakes his head.

"Stephen Small."

"I've heard the name."

The clerk explains that the Small family just sold its media empire for sixty-four million dollars. He doesn't know how much Stephen Small got, but it has to be a decent chunk. He says that Stephen Small recently bought the B. Harley Bradley House.

"You know, that fancy house over in the historic district? The one Frank Lloyd Wright designed?"

Danny knows the one.

"Some people have it all, don't they?" the clerk says, shaking his head in wonder.

"Not me," Danny groans, and tucks the measly refund into his jeans.

As he walks out the store, the manager calls after him, "Gotta make your own destiny, man."

CHAPTER 10

DANNY DRIVES AROUND, THINKING.

He has no destination in mind. He just doesn't want to go home yet. He can't stop thinking about why some people have so much and other people have so little. Why does a guy like Stephen Small get to drive around in a Ferrari and take his family out on a speedboat when Danny has to swing a hammer under the hot summer sun for meager wages?

Danny doesn't stop to consider that he was born into a life of privilege and squandered his opportunities. He focuses only on how little he has now and how his father won't even give him a loan.

It's not fair, Danny thinks.

At a stoplight, he glances in his rearview mirror and notices a black sedan two cars behind him. The windows are tinted, and he can't see the driver.

Didn't he see that car earlier today?

He can't be sure, but he thinks he spotted the car on his

way to his parents' house. He quickly takes a right, and the sedan does, too, even though its signal wasn't on while it sat at the light.

Could it be Mitch's guys?

Or the cops?

Danny takes another quick right and looks in his rearview mirror. The car rolls through the intersection without taking the turn. Danny breathes a sigh of relief, still studying the rearview mirror. He looks up in time to slam on his brakes to avoid hitting a car stopped in front of him.

Am I just being paranoid? Danny thinks.

When traffic begins moving again, Danny speeds out of the neighborhood, checking and rechecking his rearview mirror. He takes a circuitous route to make sure no one is following him anymore.

By the time he pulls up in front of the town house, Danny has made a decision.

Gotta make your own destiny, the manager had said.

Danny plans to.

He finds Nancy sitting on the couch watching a videotape of *Crocodile Dundee*. Their air conditioner isn't working, and she looks miserable in short cutoff jeans and a tight T-shirt. Her hair is damp around her forehead, and there are sweat stains on her shirt. There is fresh polish on her toenails and wads of cotton wedged between each toe.

"Honey," she says. "Do you want to go get some ice cream? It's hotter than blue blazes in this house."

"I need to run to the lumberyard," Danny says. "We can get ice cream along the way, if you'd like."

"What do you need at the lumberyard?" Nancy asks, pulling the cotton balls out from between her toes.

"I've got an idea for a new woodworking project."

"Is it something you can sell?" Nancy asks, standing up and slipping her manicured feet into a pair of flip-flops.

"Not exactly," Danny says. "But I think it could make us some money."

CHAPTER 11

WHILE DANNY IS LOOKING for the supplies he needs, Nancy wanders through the hardware store. She passes through the paint section, imagining a new color for Benji's room. Then she looks at some trim and imagines it lining the floor in their living room. She arrives at the appliance section and examines a row of dishwashers, looking at the prices. She wants badly to ask Danny if there's any way to buy a new one. Layaway? A credit card? She hates washing dishes by hand. But she knows what Danny will say.

The same thing he says when she suggests she go back to work.

No.

No, no, no!

There's no talking to him. It's always his way or the highway.

She wanders through the store, looking at faucets. They could use a new one of those too. Theirs is always leaking all over the kitchen counter. She exhales deeply, thinking about all the things she can't have.

Life had been so easy when Danny was dealing. He'd always had plenty of money for anything she wanted. Dinners in nice restaurants. Jewelry and flowers. It was a good life—much better than working two jobs before Danny came along—but it was a life that always made her feel guilty. She'd made mistakes in the past, and she liked a good party as well as the next gal, but she was trying to be a good mother. What kind of mother lets her drug-dealing boyfriend pay for the roof over her child's head?

The answer: yours truly, Nancy Rish.

The guilt had eaten her up, and she'd pushed for Danny to quit dealing. She isn't sure why he finally decided to quit, but he did. She'd initially been skeptical that he would be able to stay clean, but so far he has. It's been seven months, and times have been tough for them. But it looks like Danny isn't going to backslide to his old ways.

She tells herself she got what she wanted. She needs to be okay with washing dishes by hand and doing without the unnecessary purchases she used to make. She decides she'll tell him that they don't need to go get ice cream. She doesn't want him to stress about money. She can do without.

She finds Danny in the plumbing section talking to an employee about plastic tubing. What the hell is he planning to build?

Danny tucks three long pieces of PVC tubing under his arm and grabs a couple elbow joints. The pieces of plastic pipe flop under his arms as he walks to the front of the store. On his way, he grabs a package of caulk and a set of door hinges.

At the counter, Danny charges the purchases to his boss's account. Nancy isn't sure if Danny worked this out with his boss ahead of time. It occurs to her that it's possible that his boss purchases so many supplies at the store that he won't even notice an extra charge. She chooses to believe Danny has turned over a new leaf. She needs to stop doubting him.

As they're walking out the door, Nancy tells him that she has decided she doesn't want ice cream.

"Fine," he says, pulling the van around back to the store's lumberyard.

She wants him to recognize the sacrifice she's trying to make, but he seems too preoccupied. It hurts her feelings and she almost blurts out that she's changed her mind and wants ice cream after all. But just because Danny doesn't appreciate the sacrifice she's trying to make doesn't mean she shouldn't make it. She needs to be supportive, whether he notices or not.

Danny shows an employee his receipt. The two men load two sheets of plywood and six two-by-fours into the back of the van.

"What the heck are you building?" Nancy asks when he climbs back into the driver's seat.

"You'll see."

CHAPTER 12

NANCY DUMPS SPAGHETTI NOODLES into a pot of boiling water. The water bubbles up and spills over the side, hissing as it hits the open flame of the burner. Next to the pot on the stove is a pan of simmering marinara sauce. She dips a wooden spoon in and gives it a taste.

Satisfied, she turns to Danny, who is sitting at the kitchen table next to Benji, and says that dinner will be ready in ten minutes.

Both Benji and Danny are drawing. Using crayons, Benji is drawing a dinosaur fighting a robot. Using a mechanical pencil, Danny seems to be drawing designs for whatever it is he hopes to build. He takes a slug of his beer—his third since they got home—but doesn't take his eyes off the illustration.

Danny and Benji look cute together, both locked in concentration. Nancy's heart swells. She has long had her doubts about Danny as a father figure. But now that he is no longer dealing drugs, she feels like he could be a better role model for her son.

It is nice to see him engrossed in something. She doesn't know what the heck he is planning to build—he still hasn't told her—but it's a relief just seeing him focused on something besides how difficult life has been lately.

Curious about what he's doing, Nancy tries to sneak a peek at the drawing. He's sketched out some kind of box, with the two-by-fours serving as the frame and the plywood serving as the walls. Danny has no background in technical drawing as far as she knows, but it looks like he's done a decent job of illustrating his design. He's even included measurements for the dimensions of the box. Next to the box, he's drawn what appears to be the PVC pipe. She can't quite figure out what the PVC pipe is for. It looks like it comes out of the box, but there's nothing in the drawing to indicate what it connects to.

"Honey," Nancy says, placing her hand on Danny's shoulder, "did you hear me? Dinner's almost ready."

Danny jerks his head up, as if coming out of a trance.

"I'm not hungry," he says. "I'm going to skip dinner tonight. I want to go ahead and get started on this."

He grabs his piece of paper and rises. He opens the refrigerator and pulls out two more bottles of beer. Before heading to the garage, he stops and gives Nancy a peck on the cheek.

At first, she feels a stab of resentment. If she'd known he wasn't going to eat with them, she and Benji could have just eaten leftovers. She wants life to be as normal as possible around here. She wants them to act like a family. If Danny is running off to do something without explanation, that seems more like the Danny of old. But the kiss on the cheek—that quick act of tenderness—erases her bitterness. Despite all the pressure he's under, Danny can still take the time to make her feel special.

As she and Benji eat their spaghetti, they can hear a power saw running in the garage, biting through plywood and two-by-fours. Then Danny begins driving nails into the wood. Nancy tries to make Benji laugh by slurping her noodles up. He gives her a half-hearted smile, but he keeps looking distractedly toward the garage.

After dinner, Nancy and Benji decide to watch a movie. They turn the movie up loud so they can hear it over the racket. At some point halfway through, Nancy realizes that the banging and sawing have stopped. After she tucks Benji into bed, she goes out into the garage to investigate.

Danny is nowhere to be found.

But the box he was building is there. It's about six feet long, three feet wide, and two feet deep, with a hinged lid. The edges are caulked, so the box will be watertight, except for a two-inch hole in the lid where it looks like the PVC pipe will connect.

Nancy can't figure out what Danny could possibly mean to use it for. What is he planning to put in it?

The damn thing's big enough to hold a person.

She presses the button and raises the garage door. Danny's van is missing from the driveway. She steps out onto the concrete and looks up and down the street. The heat has finally broken, and the cool air feels refreshing. But Nancy has a sinking feeling. Again, disappearing in the middle of the night without explanation is behavior typical of the old Danny.

She forces the doubt away.

You just need to trust him, she tells herself.

CHAPTER **13**

DANNY SITS IN HIS van down the street from Stephen Small's house. His eyes are bloodshot. He has a cigarette between his lips. The van's window is open, but the smoke pools in the ceiling. Danny takes a drag and jettisons the butt out the window.

He glances around to make sure no one is watching him; then he lifts a pair of binoculars and spies the Small house. The Smalls aren't particularly careful about closing their shades at night. Danny can see into their house quite well. Through an upstairs window, he sees both parents tucking their twins into bunk beds.

Danny can't stand the look of this guy, with his receding hairline and goofy aw-shucks smile. He's probably never had a hardship in his life. His wife isn't bad-looking. Maybe a little homely. But she could do better than him, if he wasn't rich, that is. That has to be the reason she's with him.

After they tuck the boys in, they go to their other son's

room. Danny can't see well into this one, but he imagines them going through a similar ritual.

One big happy family.

It makes Danny sick.

He has two children from a previous marriage, and now Nancy wants him to be a surrogate father to her son. He loves his children, and Benji is a cute kid. But the responsibility that goes with children is just exhausting.

He had liked living in a separate house from Nancy. He was able to go back and forth between the houses whenever he wanted. It was the best of both worlds. He had a girlfriend, but he could live like a bachelor half the time. If he had Stephen Small's kind of money, he'd pay someone to tuck his kids into bed at night so he could go out and party.

After the other son's light goes out, Nancy Small heads to what Danny assumes is their bedroom. Stephen trots downstairs and appears briefly in front of the glass window on the front door. He's checking to make sure the door is locked, Danny thinks.

Stephen makes the rounds through the house, turning off lights; then he heads upstairs. He joins his wife in their bedroom and closes the curtains. Danny can't make out anything but blurs behind the white drapes. Then the lights go out. The house is dark. Quiet.

Danny moves the binoculars over the rest of the property. He studies the detached garage. To leave the house, Stephen Small has to walk from one building to the other.

Danny wonders if the side door to the garage is unlocked. He doesn't want to risk checking. There's too much at stake for him to get caught snooping around the property.

Danny starts the engine and slowly drives down the street.

He doesn't turn on his headlights until he is well past the house he's been spying on.

CHAPTER 14

September 1, 1987

NANCY SITS WITH BENJI at the kitchen table, helping him read a picture book. Their empty dinner plates have been pushed aside, and it's nearing Benji's bedtime. But school hasn't started yet, and she wants to cherish this moment. This is a new book they picked up from the library, one that's more challenging than books Benji read in the past. He needs her help as he reads.

Nancy doesn't mind helping him. In fact, she enjoys it. She has already promised that once school starts, she will help him with his homework whenever he asks. She wants to set a good example for the school year.

When they get to the last sentence, Benji looks hard and then carefully sounds out the words.

"You did it!" Nancy says, grabbing him by both shoulders.

Benji has a sheepish smile.

Nancy tells him to go put his pajamas on and brush his teeth. She'll be in to tuck him in soon.

She takes their dinner plates and scrapes the remnants into the garbage. She debates for a moment whether to let them sit in the sink overnight or wash them by hand now. The dishwasher is still broken. She takes a deep breath. No point putting it off until tomorrow.

As she's filling the sink with soapy water, she hears a noise and turns to see Danny sauntering in. She hasn't seen him all day.

"Hey, hon," she says. "There's still a little bit of dinner. Want me to make you a plate?"

He doesn't answer, and Nancy takes a moment to really look at him. His skin is flushed, and his eyes are dilated and wild. It doesn't look like he has brushed his hair in days. For that matter, it doesn't look like he's slept in days.

At first she thinks he must be high on cocaine, but she isn't sure. She's seen him stoned plenty of times, but he's never looked quite like this. He seems stressed out—to the point he's about to snap.

He opens the refrigerator and scans its contents.

"Hon," Nancy says, this time louder. "I made dinner."

"I'm not hungry," he says dismissively.

He grabs a half-full gallon of milk and walks over to the sink. He starts pouring the milk into the soapy water.

"What are you doing?" Nancy says.

She's going to have to drain the sink now and start over.

"I need some water," Danny says, as if that is explanation enough.

He begins to the fill the empty jug at the tap. The water in the container is cloudy from the milk residue.

"Danny," Nancy says softly, "is something wrong?"

"Don't worry about it," he says, without taking his eyes off the milk jug.

"You're not dealing again, are you?"

She regrets the words as soon as they come out. Danny's head jerks toward her, and he fixes her with bloodshot eyes.

"No, I'm not dealing again, goddamn it!"

He slams the jug down on the counter, and milky water sloshes out of it.

"If I was dealing again, would we have to live in this crappy little house?" he shouts. "Would we have a dishwasher that leaks all over the goddamn place?"

"I'm sorry. I just don't want you doing anything..." she says, trailing off.

"Anything what?" Danny growls. "Anything *stupid*?"

Nancy steps back. "I didn't say that."

"No, but that's what you were thinking," Danny says, leaning over her. "You think I'm stupid?"

She cowers against the countertop between the stove and the dishwasher. He raises his hand to slap her but holds back.

"You should be thankful for what I do for you," he says.

Nancy feels a burst of courage, and she stands up straight and glares at Danny with tear-filled eyes.

"Don't you love me anymore?" she says.

This snaps him from his trance. He lowers his raised hand, looking at it as if he doesn't know how it got there.

He takes a few steps back and leans against the counter, his shoulders slumped.

"I'm sorry," he says. "I'm just really stressed out right now."

Nancy takes a deep breath, steadying her voice. "Let's go to bed," she says. "You look exhausted."

"I just need a little space right now," he says, grabbing the milk jug and putting the lid back on. "I've got an errand to run."

He heads to the door, and Nancy stares at the empty space he left behind. She has the feeling of being watched. She turns to see Benji standing at the threshold of the kitchen, wearing striped pajamas. His chin quivers as he tries to stop himself from crying.

Nancy kneels and embraces him. His tiny body trembles in her arms.

"It's going to be okay," she whispers into his ear. "It's going to be okay."

She hopes her son believes her more than she believes herself.

CHAPTER 15

AFTER PUTTING BENJI TO bed, Nancy walks through the house to make sure the doors are locked. She peeks into the garage and sees that the weird box Danny built is gone. She feels a twinge of relief and isn't sure why.

She pours herself a glass of wine and goes to her bedroom. She pulls off her jeans and blouse, and she puts on one of Danny's T-shirts she uses as a nightgown. The shirt is big on her, hanging halfway down her thighs. The shirt smells of him, and the odor gives her mixed feelings. She loves him, but she knows he's not good for her.

She stands at the window and looks down onto the street. Part of her wants Danny's van to pull into the driveway. At least that way she would know he's safe. But another part of her doesn't want that. In fact, part of her hopes he never comes home again.

She crawls into bed and grabs the telephone from her bedside stand. She dials her friend Julie's number. Nancy takes a long drink of wine while she waits for Julie to answer.

"Are you okay?" Julie says right away.

Nancy opens her mouth to say yes, but she can't let the lie out.

"No," she says, and she starts to cry. "It's Danny."

"What did that bastard do to you? Did he hit you?"

"No. Nothing like that." Nancy pictures Danny raising his hand to strike her, but she doesn't tell Julie how close he came. "He's just acting really weird. He's up to something."

"Is he cheating on you?"

Nancy considers this. She wouldn't put it past him. He'd been married with two kids when he started pursuing Nancy. She'd met him at a bar, but she'd avoided him because she knew he was married. He'd been relentless and she finally gave in. They'd dated, but she wouldn't let things get serious until he started divorce proceedings.

She remembers how he'd made her feel special, how he claimed that he couldn't stay away from her. His persistence had been flattering. But times have changed. They have no money, and Danny sleeps on the couch more often than he sleeps in bed with her.

Maybe that's what this is all about. He's out there chasing women again, and he's found a new pretty young thing to replace her.

Nancy talks this theory through with Julie, but it doesn't feel right. If he was cheating, he'd probably be on his best behavior at home—not on the verge of hitting her.

"He's keeping a secret from me," Nancy says. "That's for sure. But he's still motivated to take care of me. He doesn't seem to want to leave this life with me—he just wants to make that life better."

With this statement, Nancy feels guilty for doubting him. Danny is far from perfect, but he's always had the best intentions when it comes to Nancy. She can't imagine the stress he is under. He's given up a life of crime and is struggling to make ends meet.

Julie keeps talking on the other end of the phone, but Nancy's mind is focused on that thought: he's given up a life of crime.

Nancy feels a cold chill.

Has he given up his life of crime?

CHAPTER 16

DANNY'S VAN CRAWLS THROUGH a desolate area in eastern Kankakee County known as the sand hills. Danny's headlights illuminate the sandy ground, barren except for weeds and gnarled bushes. He finds a place that looks perfect—there are no tire tracks, no footprints, no evidence that anyone comes here.

Welcome to the middle of nowhere, he thinks.

Danny climbs out of the cab and circles around to the back of the van. Inside sits the wooden box he built, the PVC pipe, a cloudy jug of water, an assortment of candy bars, a car battery, and a shovel. Danny reaches for the shovel and circles back to the front of the van, where the headlights illuminate a section of sandy ground.

Danny stabs the blade of his shovel into the loose dirt. He tosses a shovelful of sand aside. Then another. And another. Particles of dust float in the headlight beams. He works hard, breaking a sweat. His hands start to ache. He takes a break to smoke a cigarette and then gets back at it.

When the hole is big enough, he turns the van around and backs up to it. He grabs ahold of the box and drags it out. It fits snugly in the hole. Once he shovels the dirt back on top, there will be a good two feet of earth between the box and the outside world.

Danny puts the car battery into the box, along with the water jug and the candy bars. He closes the lid and admires his craftsmanship—and his plan.

But Danny isn't done yet. He takes the shovel and begins scraping a trench in the dirt, starting from the hole and working his way toward a cluster of weeds about twenty-five feet away. Once he's satisfied with the trough, he takes the PVC tubes out of the van and begins connecting them. He lays them in place and then shovels back over the trench until the only pipe visible is a stub sticking into the hole that he will connect to the lid once he seals the box. The other end of the air tube is hidden in the weeds.

Danny sits in the back of the van and lights a cigarette. His hands are filthy, his shirt sweat-stained.

To the east, the dark horizon is beginning to turn blue with the first hints of sunrise.

Danny smiles to himself. *It's a good plan,* he thinks. *It's going to work.*

CHAPTER 17

September 2

NANCY WAKES UP TO the sound of the shower. Warm sunlight floods the room. She sits up and notices that a cup of coffee and a doughnut are sitting on her nightstand.

Danny comes out with a towel around his waist, his hair wet and dripping. He smiles and gives her a firm kiss on the lips. She looks at him skeptically. Does he not remember what happened last night?

"I've got an idea," he says, more chipper than she's seen him in months. "After we drop off Benji at his dad's, let's go for a drive. We can go look at horses."

Nancy can't help but smile. She loves taking drives and looking at horse ranches. She's tempted to stop him and say they need to talk about what happened last night, but Danny seems to want to move past it. She decides to let it go. He's under a lot of pressure, and this is his gesture of making amends.

Thirty minutes later, they're zooming out of town

toward the countryside. Danny whistles. Nancy lets her hand dance in the breeze. They pass farms and horse paddocks, and Nancy feels relaxed. They don't need a lot of money. All they need is each other and a nice scenic drive—when Danny isn't acting weird, that is.

They're approaching the area known as the sand hills, where the vegetation isn't as lush. Danny pulls over next to a railroad crossing. He parks the car in a pullout, and Nancy has the thought that he's going to lean over and kiss her, the way he used to when they couldn't keep their hands off each other.

Instead, he looks her in the eyes, suddenly serious, and says, "Do you know where we are? Could you find this place if you came back without me?"

Nancy nods, uncertain what's going on.

"I need you to do me a favor," Danny says. "I need you to pick me up here at three o'clock tonight."

"Three o'clock?" she says, incredulous. "In the morning?"

"Yes."

Nancy feels sick. All morning she'd been thinking he'd turned over a new leaf. Things were finally going to change. But he is up to something.

"This whole morning wasn't so we could spend time together," she says, hurt. "You've got some kind of scheme going on, and you're trying to rope me into it."

Danny looks at her sincerely. "Listen, Nancy. I need you to do this for me. Don't ask me why, but I'll need a ride from this place at three o'clock."

Nancy looks out her window, thinking. They're in the

middle of nowhere. She can't imagine what Danny will be doing here in the middle of the night.

Unless he's making a drug deal.

"You promised me that you were done with anything shady," she says.

"Just this last thing," Danny says. "I have to do this, and then I promise I'm done forever."

"Just tell me one thing," she says. "Is it drugs? Are you dealing again?"

Danny takes her hand in his and looks earnestly into her eyes.

"I promise I am not dealing drugs," he says.

"Okay," she says, taking a deep, nervous breath. "I'll do it."

As they drive away, the mood in the car has changed. Danny seems agitated again, stressed. Nancy is quiet. She tries to convince herself that as long as Danny isn't dealing, then whatever he's up to can't be too bad.

It doesn't occur to her that it might be worse.

CHAPTER 18

STEPHEN SMALL AND HIS wife, Nancy, sit in their bed talking about plans for the upcoming Labor Day weekend. It will be the kids' last big hurrah before school starts again, and they want to make it memorable. As they wrap up their conversation, Stephen leans over, kisses Nancy good night, and then takes off his glasses and sets them on the nightstand. He reaches to turn off the lamp, but stops. Downstairs, the telephone begins to ring.

"Who is calling at this hour?" Stephen says.

It's after midnight.

Stephen pulls his legs out from under the comforter and slides his feet into a pair of slippers. The phone stops ringing.

"Ramsey got it," Nancy Small says. "He's up watching a movie, remember. It's probably one of his friends."

Stephen is putting his legs back under the blanket when Ramsey knocks gently on the door and pokes his head into the room.

"Dad," the fifteen-year-old says. "The police are on the phone."

"The police?" Stephen says.

"Yeah. He said he needs to talk to you. Said it's important."

Stephen gives Nancy a perplexed look and then heads downstairs to the phone.

"This is Stephen Small," he says. "How may I help you?"

"Sir," says a male voice, "I hate to bother you at this hour, but there's been a break-in at the Bradley House. You own the house, correct? The one in the historic district?"

"Yes," Stephen says, his heart pounding.

"We've caught the intruders," says the voice on the other end. "We've got them at the Kankakee Police Station. But we need you to come down to the Bradley House and assess the scene, see if there's any damage or anything missing we don't know about."

"Of course," Stephen says. "I'll be right there."

He hangs up the phone and jogs up the stairs.

"I've got to run down to the Bradley House," he tells his wife. "Apparently someone broke in."

He explains that the perpetrators have been caught, but the police need him to take a look at the house and make sure everything is okay.

Stephen pulls on a pair of blue jeans and a T-shirt. He slips his feet into a pair of loafers and grabs his eyeglasses off the nightstand.

"I love you," he says, kissing Nancy on the cheek.

"Be careful," his wife says.

Stephen hurries through the yard toward the detached

garage. He unlocks the side door and steps inside. He presses the button to raise the garage door. When he opens the door to his Mercedes, he catches movement out of the corner of his eye.

A dark figure ducks under the opening garage door and bounds to the side of the Mercedes. He points a gun directly between Stephen's eyes.

Stephen can't see the armed man's face. It's covered with a motorcycle helmet. Stephen looks at his own terrified reflection in the helmet's visor.

"What's this all about?" Stephen says, his voice trembling.

"We're going for a ride," says the man with the gun.

His voice is muffled because of the motorcycle helmet, but Stephen still recognizes it. The voice is the same one he just spoke to on the telephone.

CHAPTER 19

September 3

DRIVING HIS MERCEDES WHILE the mysterious man sits behind him, Stephen has trouble gripping the steering wheel because his hands are shaking so much. The back of his T-shirt is soaked with sweat.

The streets of Kankakee are empty, the shops closed up for the night. Stephen keeps hoping he'll see a police car and be able to get the officer's attention somehow. But there's no one around. The streetlights illuminate vacant parking lots, storefronts with their lights turned off, empty sidewalks along the roadway.

Stephen checks the rearview mirror to look at his kidnapper. He notices the man has a ski mask underneath the helmet. Whoever he is, he's gone out of his way to disguise his identity, which gives Stephen a flicker of hope. If the man planned to kill him, he wouldn't have bothered hiding his face. At least Stephen hopes that's the case.

"I'm a rich man," Stephen says. "I can give you money, if you just let me go."

"I know you're rich," the kidnapper says, but that's all.

Stephen drives for a minute without speaking, and then he decides to try again.

"What are you going to do?"

"If you don't shut up," the man says, lifting the gun and aiming it at the back of Stephen's head, "I'm going to splatter your goddamn brains all over the windshield."

Stephen's breath catches in his throat. He feels his insides constrict.

"Turn here," the man says, and Stephen does as he's told.

They pass the *Welcome to Kankakee* sign and head out of town. Soon the residential streets turn to rural countryside. There are no streetlights, just patches of forest and fences lining pastureland.

The kidnapper tells Stephen to pull off the paved road onto a dirt road. Soon after, he directs Stephen to leave the dirt road altogether, and Stephen finds himself navigating around trees and brush and patches of weeds.

Stephen's hands start shaking even more. He thought the man didn't plan to kill him, but what other purpose could he have for bringing him out to the middle of nowhere? This is the perfect place to bury a body.

"If you kill me," Stephen blurts out, "you won't get your money. I'm rich. I can pay you. Please just let me go."

"Calm down," the voice behind the helmet says, sounding much more relaxed than he did while they were in the city. "Everything's going to be fine. I've worked out all the details. You're not going to die."

"Then let me go."

"Not just yet," the man says. "Stop here."

Stephen parks the car, its headlights illuminating nothing but sandy, weed-filled ground. Stephen starts to shake uncontrollably.

"Turn off the lights," the man says.

Stephen presses the button, and then the two of them are sitting in blackness.

"Shut the engine off."

Stephen can hardly grip the key because of his trembling hands, but he finally gets his fingers to cooperate.

"Hand the keys to me."

Stephen reaches behind him, and the man takes the keys.

"Now get out of the car," the man instructs him. "If you want to tuck your kids into bed or kiss your wife good night ever again, you'll do exactly as I tell you."

CHAPTER 20

THE MASKED MAN ORDERS Stephen to hold out his arms and then clips a pair of handcuffs around his wrists, squeezing the metal rings tight against his skin.

"Walk," the man orders, pressing the barrel of the pistol against Stephen's lower back.

Stephen staggers forward. The moon is out, but it's far from full, casting barely enough light for Stephen to see by. He isn't dressed for this kind of cross-country trek. His loafers quickly fill with dirt. It's a hot, muggy night, and Stephen's skin is sticky with sweat. He hears insects chirruping, and somewhere in the darkness a bullfrog croaks.

The man follows a pace behind, holding the gun in one hand and carrying a duffel bag with his other arm.

"Please," Stephen says, turning his head slightly to look at the man over his shoulder. "Whatever you're planning, you don't have to do it. I've already told you I'll give you money."

"I'll get my money, all right," the man says, poking Stephen with the gun again.

Stephen jerks as if he's been burned by a hot poker. His foot collides with a clump of dirt and he stumbles forward, landing on his hands and knees. His glasses slip off his sweaty face and fall into a patch of weeds. He gropes for his glasses with his cuffed hands, but his kidnapper grabs him by the back of the shirt and yanks him to his feet.

"Wait," Stephen says. "My glasses."

"You'll buy another pair," the man growls, shoving Stephen.

Stephen almost falls again, but he catches himself. Without his glasses, the world is a blur. Between the darkness and his own impaired vision, he can make out almost nothing, just clumps of vegetation or the occasional tree.

"Stop here," the man orders.

Stephen squints. He can make out a large discoloration in the sandy ground in front of him. It looks like a large hole in the dirt. Stephen hunches over and tries to look more closely.

He sees an open coffin sitting in the hole.

"No," Stephen says, wheeling around and collapsing to his knees. "Please don't kill me. I have a wife, three kids. They need me."

"Shut up," the voice says, sounding annoyed. "I'm not going to kill you. There's a breathing tube. As long as your family does what they're supposed to do, you're going to live. Okay? Relax."

The kidnapper orders Stephen to stand in the box. Then the man removes a handheld tape recorder from the duffel bag and hands Stephen a handwritten note. He points a small flashlight onto the text.

"Read the words as they're written," the man orders, and he presses record.

Stephen squints again. Without his glasses, he can barely make out the words.

The man presses the gun barrel against Stephen's skull and nods his head toward the note.

"Nancy, this is, this is, umm, this...I...that...I thought this was a joke or something, but it's no joke. I'm...there's somebody and I've got handcuffs on, and I'm inside some, I guess, a box."

Danny interrupts: "You got two days of air and that's it. And it's going to get real stuffy in there."

Stephen can make out enough of the note to relay the kidnapper's demands to Nancy. He says to get 1 million dollars in fifty- and hundred-dollar bills. No consecutive serial numbers.

"You've got forty-eight hours of air," the man says, speaking toward the microphone.

"I love you," Stephen says. "I really do, and the kids. That's all I know. This hurts like hell."

The masked man presses the stop button and puts the recorder back in his bag, then pulls out bolt cutters and severs the chain between the handcuffs. The kidnapper points out the amenities inside the box: There are candy bars, light, water, and even an air tube.

"I'll be back out as soon as your family ponies up."

"You don't have to do this," Stephen says as he first kneels and then lies down in the box.

The man slams the lid closed. Then he adjusts the air tube sticking through the plywood.

Stephen calls out to his kidnapper, telling him it's not too late to let him go.

The kidnapper says nothing. He answers by throwing a shovelful of dirt on top of the box. Stephen cries for help as dirt rains down onto the lid. He tries to shift positions, but it's almost impossible to move—and the temperature inside the box is sweltering.

He feels like he can't catch his breath, and he strains his neck toward the air hole. In doing so, he knocks the car battery and the light flickers. He feels on the verge of panic.

This can't be happening.

He adjusts the battery. At least he has light now, but he can't control his breathing. He gets his mouth as close to the air hole as he can and tries to take slow, deep inhalations through the pipe.

The wooden roof starts to sag under the weight of the dirt.

CHAPTER 21

NANCY RISH WAITS FOR Danny at the railroad crossing, as she was instructed. She looks around, nervous, unsure if whatever Danny is up to is illegal. She thinks about firing up the engine and driving away, leaving Danny to whatever trouble he's gotten himself into this time.

But she can't bring herself to do it. She loves him. She wants a life with him.

A normal life.

Is this a normal life? she asks herself. *Waiting by a railroad track in the middle of nowhere at three in the morning? No, this is far from a normal life.*

But Danny has promised this is the last time he'll do something like this. And at least it—whatever *it* is—is not drug dealing.

Even if this isn't a normal life, maybe a normal life is right around the corner. A little voice inside Nancy's head tells her she's just fooling herself. But she's already here, already waiting. What would Danny do if she drove off without him?

He almost slapped her the other day. Whatever he is into is stressing him out to the point that he was almost willing to hurt her.

It probably wouldn't be a good idea to abandon Danny now. If she did, she might as well go home and grab Benji out of bed and run away. But where could she go?

The answer is simple: nowhere.

If she runs away from Danny, she has nowhere to run to.

She bites her fingernails and looks around impatiently.

Danny comes walking toward the car, emerging from the darkness like a phantom. He is carrying a duffel bag slung over his shoulder.

Nancy scowls at him as he opens the door.

"There aren't any drugs in there, are there?"

"No," Danny says, irritated. "I already told you I'm not dealing."

"Then what are you doing?"

Danny leans his head back against the headrest like he's worn out from a hard day's work.

"You don't want to know," he mutters.

Danny is filthy. His pant legs are dusty, and his hands are caked in what looks like a muddy mix of dirt and sweat.

Nancy opens her mouth to speak, but Danny cuts her off with a curt "Let's get going already."

Nancy starts the engine and drives away. The headlights

slice through the darkness. They drive in silence for several minutes.

"Pull over up here," Danny says, pointing to a gas station. "I need to make a phone call."

"At this hour?"

Danny doesn't answer, and Nancy doesn't press him. She pulls off into the gravel parking lot and stops the car. She leans back and closes her eyes as she waits.

She doesn't see Danny pull a tape recorder out of the duffel bag when he gets to the pay phone.

CHAPTER 22

September 3
3:00 a.m.

NANCY SMALL IS ASLEEP and dreaming when she hears a telephone ringing. She sits up, looks around, tries to orient herself. She's sitting in a recliner in the living room. She sat down to wait for Stephen to return home and ended up dozing off.

Now she checks the clock in the kitchen and sees how late it is. The phone is still ringing. She hurries and grabs it.

"Hello," she says.

"Nancy," she hears her husband say, but his voice is distorted, muffled. It's hard to hear him, but the voice is still recognizable as her husband's. *"This is, this is, umm, this…I…that…I thought this was a joke or something, but it's no joke. I'm…there's somebody and I've got handcuffs on, and I'm inside some, I guess, a box."*

Nancy's mind reels as she tries to keep up with what Stephen is saying.

He's locked in a box?

I'm supposed to come up with a million dollars?

"Slow down," she says. "What is going on?"

She hears another voice, even more distorted, say something about forty-eight hours of air. Then she hears Stephen's voice again.

"I love you. I really do, and the kids. That's all I know. This hurts like hell."

"Wait, Stephen—"

Another voice comes on the line.

"We have your husband."

This voice isn't distorted or muffled. It's clear and cold, and hearing it sends chills down Nancy Small's spine.

"Get the money together," the voice says. "If you don't give me one million, your husband is dead."

"I don't know if I can get that kind of money," Nancy pleads.

"Your husband is buried in a box, and only I know where it is," the voice says. "He has forty-eight hours of air. If I don't get what I want, I'll leave him there to rot. You'll never find him."

"I need some time."

"I'll call back," the voice says. "And don't you dare go to the cops."

The line goes dead.

Nancy's heart is jackhammering in her chest. Tears fill her eyes. She paces the room for a moment, trying to process what is happening.

She considers not calling the police, trying to do this alone. Could she assemble that kind of money? Could she do what the caller asks in exchange for Stephen?

There is no guarantee that Stephen will be allowed to live. She only has the kidnapper's word, and she can't trust him.

No, Stephen's best chance of survival is for her to call in the authorities.

She grabs the phone and dials the operator.

She clears her throat and says in as confident a voice as she can muster, "Please connect me to the FBI."

CHAPTER 23

IN THE LATE MORNING, Danny Edwards cruises down the residential street where Stephen and Nancy Small live. He is driving slowly, trying to look for anything suspicious, but also trying not to look suspicious himself. Everything seems normal. A man is trimming his lawn with a push mower. A teenager is riding his bike. An elderly woman is kneeling in a planter of flowers, clipping roses.

Danny pulls over near the Small house and pretends to consult a piece of paper. Really, he's looking around for evidence of law enforcement. He doesn't see any marked cars or uniformed officers. The Small house looks like it does any other day, except the blinds are pulled and there are no kids running around in the yard playing in the sprinkler.

Danny is about to put the van in drive when he sees one of the curtains shift. A man in a suit looks out, glances around, and then pulls the curtain shut again.

"Damn her," Danny growls, firing up the engine and speeding down the street. "That bitch called the goddamn cops."

Danny heads out of town, careful to make sure he isn't followed. He drives to the sand hills, finds the spot where Stephen Small pulled off the road last night, and follows the tire tracks.

The Mercedes is just where he left it, hidden in a cluster of bushes and trees. He keeps going and pulls up to the place he buried Stephen Small. It's easy to see that the dirt has been disturbed here, but because the air tube sticks out of the ground twenty feet away, Danny doesn't think anyone who might wander upon the spot would think that a person is buried alive down there.

He heads over to the place where the pipe is sticking out of the ground. The sunlight seems unusually bright and oppressive. The air is hot and humid. A mosquito buzzes around his ear, and he swats it away.

Danny leans over the tube sticking out of the ground and calls out, "Hang in there, man. This is almost over."

He stops and listens for Stephen Small to say something.

"Stephen, you in there, buddy?"

There is no response.

Danny opens his mouth to call out to Stephen again, but he hears something in the brush nearby. He freezes and stares. He sees no movement. Was it a bird? A rabbit?

Or something else?

You're just being paranoid, he tells himself. *Keep it together.*

He hurries back to his van and spins the tires in the

sand trying to get out of there. When he gets to the blacktop, he keeps looking around, checking his rearview mirrors.

Is someone following him?

He doesn't see anyone who looks suspicious, but he just can't shake the feeling that he's being spied on.

Maybe this is how I'll feel the rest of my life, he thinks. *Like someone is after me.*

CHAPTER 24

September 3
5:00 p.m.

FOURTEEN HOURS AFTER SHE first talked to her husband's kidnapper, Nancy Small's phone begins to ring.

Everyone in the house—the Kankakee police, the FBI, her lawyer—all go quiet. One of the FBI agents gives Nancy a nod.

She looks at the recording device next to her phone, trying to remember how they told her to operate it. She presses the record button and slowly lifts the receiver.

"Hello," she says, attempting to sound as calm as possible.

"I told you not to call the cops," the voice on the other end growls. "Do you want your husband to die?"

Nancy inhales sharply. Tears spring to her eyes. She tells herself to remain calm.

"I have the money," she says coolly.

This statement seems to relax the man a bit.

"How much?" he says.

"All of it—one million," she says. "It's in hundreds and fifties, no sequential serial numbers. Just as you asked."

"I'll call you back with instructions," the man says.

One of the FBI agents gestures to Nancy with his hands: *Keep him on the phone.*

"I want to talk to my husband," Nancy says, her voice beginning to lose its composure for the first time.

"You called the police," the man snaps. "You messed everything up. It's more complicated now. I'll call you back."

"I want to talk to Stephen," she pleads, her voice breaking.

There's no answer. The line is dead.

Nancy Small lowers the phone to its cradle. Her hand is shaking. Her whole body is numb.

The head FBI agent in charge puts a gentle, reassuring hand on her shoulder.

"You did good," he says. "We traced the call."

Relief floods through Nancy's body.

The agents start frantically discussing what to do. The call came from a pay phone at a Phillips 66 gas station in Aroma Park, about thirty miles outside of Kankakee.

"I want four stakeout teams," the agent in charge says. "One for that gas station and three more for the closest pay phones. The next time the kidnapper makes a call, we're going to pounce on that son of a bitch."

CHAPTER 25

September 3
11:00 p.m.

NANCY RISH AND DANNY EDWARDS are sitting on the couch, watching the rest of *Crocodile Dundee*. Nancy sneaks a glance at Danny, who can't sit still. He keeps looking toward the window and his leg keeps fidgeting. His skin seems flush, and she can tell he isn't paying attention to the movie. His eyes might be looking at the TV screen, but his mind is a million miles away.

"Are you okay?" Nancy asks.

He doesn't say anything.

"Danny?"

"I'm fine," he snaps.

After a few minutes, the telephone rings, and Danny jumps out of his seat as if he's heard a gunshot.

"What is going on with you?" Nancy says, walking toward the phone stand. "Hello?" She holds the receiver to her chest and says to Danny, "It's Julie."

She sits down and begins talking to her friend. Julie wants to know what her plans are for Labor Day weekend.

Danny's legs bounce restlessly. Finally, he bursts out of his seat and storms out of the house.

"Is Danny still acting weird?" Julie says.

"Weirder than ever," Nancy says.

After a long conversation about everything from Benji's school clothes to the weather, Nancy finally hangs up. She goes looking for Danny. He isn't anywhere in the house. She peeks into the garage and sees him pacing around. She opens her mouth to ask what he's doing when he spots her.

"Hey," he says, excited. "I've got an idea."

Nancy looks at him skeptically as he explains. Since Benji is at his dad's tonight, Danny says, they should take Nancy's bicycle over to his friend Jerry's house to get the brakes fixed.

"At this hour?"

"He's a night owl," Danny says. "He won't mind."

Without waiting for a response, Danny opens the garage door and wheels the ten-speed into the driveway.

"Let's take your car," he says. "We'll put the bike in the trunk."

Nancy steps out onto the driveway in bare feet. The night air is muggy. Danny is trying to wedge her bicycle into the trunk. The brakes haven't worked in months. Every time she mentioned getting the bike fixed to Danny, he said he had a friend who could do the work. But he never got around to calling him and asking for the favor. It seemed to be the lowest item on his priority list. She can't imagine why, at eleven o'clock tonight, he unexpectedly wants to get this done.

"Danny," she says, "what's really going on?"

Danny can't get the trunk closed, so he leaves it ajar, with the handlebars sticking out.

"I just want to go for a drive with my girl," he says. "And I thought we'd get an errand done while we're at it."

She purses her lips and folds her arms, trying with her body language to send the message that she doesn't believe a word he's saying.

"Nancy," he says, putting his hands on her shoulders. "I've told you a hundred times. I'm not dealing anymore. I've learned my lesson. I've got a second chance, and I'm not going to blow it."

Then he wraps his arms around her in a tight hug and adds, "Besides, I would never put you in a situation where you could get in trouble for something I've done. Trust me, okay?"

She doesn't answer. She wraps her arms around him and sinks into his embrace, and that says it all.

CHAPTER 26

NANCY DRIVES HER BUICK on the same route they'd gone the other day when they were looking at the scenery, and then again last night when she picked Danny up at three o'clock in the morning. Her bicycle is poking out of the open trunk, rattling around behind them.

Danny isn't talking. He's fidgeting in his seat, just as he was at home.

So much for our nice evening drive as a couple, Nancy thinks.

"Pull over here," Danny says. "Let me call Jerry, just to make sure it's okay if we swing by."

"You said he's a night owl."

"He is. I just want to make sure he's there."

Nancy eases the car into the gravel driveway of a bait shop, and she parks near the pay phone. She turns off the engine. There's no telling how long Danny will be.

Danny hops out and looks around. The shop is closed. There are signs in the windows written in Magic Marker advertising fresh worms and inexpensive fishing lures, but the store itself is dark. The neon Budweiser sign is turned off. The parking lot is lit only from a single streetlight. There are no other cars in the lot. Danny looks up and down the road and sees no headlights. He listens and hears only crickets and the rustling of tree leaves.

He dials the number of Nancy Small.

"Hello," the woman says after two rings.

"Take Route 17 east," Danny says.

"What?" she says. "Wait. I want to talk to my husband."

Danny continues giving directions, telling her to leave the money by the railroad tracks where he had Nancy pick him up the other night. But the woman can't keep up and asks him to repeat what he said.

"Wait a minute," she says, her voice panicked. "I'm not getting this."

CHAPTER 27

AS NANCY SMALL PLEADS with her husband's kidnapper over the telephone, the police and FBI whisper to each other in the background.

"We've traced the call to Aroma Park," someone reports to the special agent in charge.

"We've heard from all four stakeouts," another agent says. "No one is using any of the phones."

"How is that possible?" someone asks.

"There must be another phone in the area."

The special agent in charge has a radio in his hand with a surveillance team on the other end.

"We spotted one more pay phone down the road," the surveillance officer says, his voice crackling through the radio.

"Go check it out," the agent in charge says. "Go, go, go!"

On the telephone, Nancy Small is still trying to make sure she understands the directions correctly.

"I'm not getting this," she says, panic overtaking her voice.

Then she hears another voice on the phone. It takes her a moment to realize it's her husband's voice, muffled and distorted again like it was the other night.

"*If everything is okay,*" Stephen says, "*if he gets the money, he'll tell you where I'm buried. He seems serious.*"

"*I'm not doing this for nothing,*" the other voice says. Now it is distorted too. "*I'm not coming back to dig you up. If I don't get my money, you're dead.*"

Nancy opens her mouth to call out to her husband, but before she can speak, the line goes dead.

She collapses to the floor, weeping loudly, relieved to know Stephen is still alive.

She doesn't realize that his voice was on a tape recorder.

CHAPTER 28

DANNY PRESSES STOP ON the tape player and hangs up the phone. His whole body feels tense. He turns back to the Buick, and just as he does, he sees a black sedan driving down the road. It has a large antenna sticking up from the trunk, and it looks a lot like an unmarked police car. Danny should know—he spent some time in them when he was working with the Kankakee drug-enforcement agents last winter.

"Goddammit," Danny mutters, and hurries to Nancy's car.

"Let's go," he says, practically shouting. "Come on. Come on!"

"Jeez," she says. "What's wrong with you?"

Danny doesn't answer.

The sedan slowly passes the bait shop. Once the car has passed, Danny watches as it attempts a three-point turn in the middle of the road.

"Was Jerry home?" Nancy asks.

"He can't do it," Danny snaps. "Go this way. Hurry up."

Nancy drives the Buick onto the road. Danny watches in the rearview mirror as the car begins to follow them. He checks and rechecks the mirror, squirming in his seat as if it's a bed of nails.

The car is behind them, its headlights far away but clearly visible. But then the car turns off the road, and the lights disappear.

Danny collapses into his seat.

"Sorry," he says. "It just seemed like that car was follow-ing us."

"You're being paranoid," Nancy says. "Why would any-one be following us?"

Danny has an idea. He sits up and rolls down his win-dow and zips open the duffel bag.

"Keep your eyes on the road," he says to Nancy.

"What are you talking about?" she says, but she keeps her eyes forward, fixed on the yellow lines in the center of the road.

Danny pulls out the tape recorder and launches it out the window into the weeds. Then he rolls up the window and sinks back into his seat, exhaling loudly.

"Are you going to tell me what the hell is going on?" Nancy says.

"I'm telling you for the last time, Nancy. For your own good, stop asking so many goddamn questions."

Nancy says nothing more, just keeps driving. She doesn't know what Danny has gotten himself into—and doesn't want to know.

When she passes another gas station up on her left, there is a car sitting in the lot, waiting to pull out. When she passes the car, she looks out her window and, under a parking lot lamp, makes eye contact with a woman behind the wheel.

The car pulls onto the road behind Nancy's Buick and begins following them at a distance.

CHAPTER 29

NANCY SMALL SITS ON the couch, her legs pulled up underneath her, her arms wrapped tightly around her body. It's as if she's trying to become smaller, squeezing into as tiny a space as possible. The room is dark except for a pool of light cast by a reading lamp next to her. The windows in the room are curtained, but the darkness outside seems to press against the house. She can't wait for the sun to rise. Somehow she associates the dawn with an end to this nightmare she's living.

This is the couch she normally shares with her family. She sits on one end, Stephen the other, and the boys—all three of them—squeeze in between them. Now the couch is empty. She's in her normal spot, but the boys are staying with her parents. And Stephen...she doesn't know where Stephen is.

No one does.

At least no one besides his kidnapper.

Their house—their warm house that holds memories

in every corner—is now full of FBI agents and police detectives.

It's the middle of the night, and no one has slept, least of all Nancy Small.

Her mind is a fog. To her, the men in suits are just blurs in the background. They move around doing whatever they're doing, but her mind is elsewhere.

She is trying to remember the last time she saw Stephen. He left in a hurry, running out of the house because he believed there had been a break-in at the B. Harley Bradley House. She can't remember if she said she loved him as he was walking out the door. Or if he said it to her.

It was their habit to say the words whenever they parted, but he'd been in such a hurry to get out the door, they might have forgotten.

It seems very important to remember whether she said it or not. She wants to remember Stephen's face as he said the words.

She shakes her head, trying to clear it of her spiraling thoughts.

But then she notices something is different in the house. The atmosphere has changed. The police officers are talking with more urgency, speaking into radios, discussing what to do. Their voices are louder as they call out ideas to each other.

Nancy wants to ask what's happening, but she feels paralyzed on the couch. How can she inquire about what's going on when she can't even rise to her feet?

Finally, the agent who seems to be in charge—she's

forgotten his name—approaches her and sits gently on the couch next to her, where Ramsey usually sits. The FBI agent wears round glasses and has a paunch. He looks like a nice man, and, from the start, she has believed him when he told her that he will do everything he can to bring her husband home safe.

"Nancy," he says. "We've caught a break."

"Do you know where Stephen is?"

"Not yet," he says, "but we're getting close."

He explains that the surveillance teams spotted a car leaving the location where the telephone call was made. An undercover officer followed the car to a home in Kankakee.

"We've run the plates," he says. "Does the name Nancy Rish mean anything to you?"

Nancy is stunned for a moment—the absurdity that Stephen's kidnapper is a woman with the same first name as hers? Then she thinks hard, traveling through her mind looking for any reference to the name.

"No," she says. "I have no idea who that is."

"Well," the agent says, "we believe she is one of the kidnappers, working with at least one accomplice. We're assembling a SWAT team now. We're going to bring her down. If all goes well, we'll have Stephen home by dinner tomorrow."

Nancy feels her heart swell with hope. But then a cold needle pops her balloon of optimism, and she fills back up with apprehension.

The kidnapper said Stephen had forty-eight hours of air.

If he isn't home by dinner, as the agent suggested, then he'll soon be running out of oxygen.

CHAPTER 30

NANCY RISH IS DREAMING.

In the dream, Benji is graduating from high school. She is sitting in the stands with Danny. They're older. Danny's hair is going gray at the temples. She's put on a little bit of weight and has a few wrinkles around her eyes. But she's still pretty. And they are happy together.

There's a gold wedding band on Danny's ring finger and a pea-sized diamond on hers. As Benji takes the stage and receives his diploma, Danny reaches over and takes her hand. They smile. This is it: the life she always wanted.

Then a loud noise—like a car crashing into the house—jolts her awake. She sits up, trying to orient herself to where she is. She's in her bed. The room is dark, but the curtains of her window are pulled back, casting a bluish light into the room. The sun isn't up yet, but it's close. She can tell by the soft morning glow.

She feels for Danny in the space next to her. He's not there.

She hears yelling coming from downstairs. Lots of voices—deep and loud and full of authority. Danny's voice, defiant but scared, is mixed in with the other voices.

Nancy's first thought is that the drug dealers Danny used to work for have come for him and they're going to kill him.

She is frozen with fear, unable to get up.

She thinks of Benji. She must protect him. Then she remembers that he is at his father's.

Thank God, she thinks.

But her relief is short-lived. Loud footsteps stomp up the stairway. The bedroom door bursts open, slamming against the wall. Nancy jumps and lets out a short, clipped scream.

Two men step into the room. They're dressed in black, with combat boots and bullet-proof vests. Both are holding military rifles, and they aim them at Nancy's face.

"Danny!" Nancy screams.

She doesn't know what else to do.

She gets no answer from Danny.

Instead, one of the SWAT agents pulls her to her feet. He is forceful but doesn't hurt her.

"Ma'am," he says. "You can put on some clothes before we take you in."

Clothes? she thinks. *Take me in?*

She doesn't understand what is going on.

She looks down at herself and sees she's wearing Danny's T-shirt, the one she uses as a nightgown. She has no bra, no underwear.

She looks around the room, trying to find some clothes to wear. She grabs a pair of jeans lying on the floor. Then something out the window catches her eye.

She walks to the edge of the window and looks out. The road is filled with police cars. Blue and red lights flash in the dim morning light. Two officers dressed like the ones in her room are leading Danny across the lawn to a police vehicle. His hands are cuffed behind his back.

A female officer arrives in the bedroom and keeps an eye on Nancy as she gets dressed. Nancy pulls on the pair of jeans and puts on a blouse. The officer is wearing street clothes and her black hair is in a ponytail, but she has a pistol clipped to her belt. Nancy thinks she looks familiar. She just isn't sure from where.

Then it hits her like a bucket of cold water dumped over her head. She saw the woman last night driving the car that was behind them.

Danny was right. They were being followed. Now Nancy is more confused than ever.

"Can you at least tell me what's going on?" Nancy says.

The woman answers by instructing Nancy to put her hands behind her back. The woman clips on handcuffs and leads her down the stairs and into the yard. Blue and red lights flash from the police cars.

The garage door is open, and police are inside, looking around. One uniformed officer is standing before a man in a suit, showing him a sawed-off hunk of two-by-four and a short length of PVC tubing. Two plainclothes detectives are kneeling over Danny's duffel bag. They pull out a motorcycle helmet Nancy has never seen before. Then a pair of bolt cutters. A flashlight.

Finally, one man pulls out a pistol. He holds it between his thumb and forefinger, like it's something he doesn't want to touch.

"Someone tell me what's going on," Nancy says, practically shouting.

"As if you don't know," the female officer says, opening the back of a police cruiser and gesturing for her to get in.

CHAPTER 31

THEY PUT NANCY IN a room with cinder-block walls and into a cold metal chair in front of a stained metal table. On the other side is another chair that sits empty.

For now.

"I want to see Danny," she says. "I think we can clear up this misunderstanding if I can just see him."

Instead of answering, they slam the heavy steel door on her. She tries the handle.

Locked.

She settles into her chair. The room is so silent she can hear her own heartbeat. The room has a dankness to it, like an underground basement. The air has the faint sour smell of body odor. And perhaps there's the stink of urine.

Nancy doesn't know how long she can stand being in here. Panic starts to creep through her bloodstream.

Thank God Benji wasn't home, she thinks.

But this thought leads to another thought. She needs to get out of here before Benji comes home from his dad's.

She wonders how long this will take before whatever has led to her mistaken arrest becomes clear.

She hears the bolt slide free, and the door swings open. She feels relieved to know they're not going to make her wait. That must be a good sign, right? That they're not going to make her sweat before talking to her?

But as the agents walk into the room, the expressions on their faces quell her relief. These men are tired and haggard, with loose ties and circles under their eyes.

The first man, who settles into the chair across from Nancy, has sideburns and a pair of circular eyeglasses. Under ordinary circumstances, he would probably look like a very nice man, but right now he looks like someone you wouldn't want to cross. The other man has a mustache and is going bald. Both men have five-o'clock shadows, and their suits hang from their bodies like they haven't been changed in a couple days.

"I'm going to make this really easy on you, Nancy," the one with the glasses says to her. "Where is Stephen Small?"

Nancy looks back and forth between him and the other man, who leans against the wall with his arms crossed.

"Who?" she says.

The agent slams his palm down on the metal table and makes Nancy jump.

"Don't play stupid with me!" he snaps. "A man's life is at stake. Don't you understand that?"

His actions are so rapid that his glasses slide down his nose. He pushes them back up the bridge of his nose with his index finger.

"Stephen Small?" Nancy says. "You mean the millionaire?"

"That's who you kidnapped, isn't it?"

"No, no, wait," Nancy says, shaking her head. "There's some kind of misunderstanding. Kidnapped? What is going on?"

Nancy knows who Stephen Small is, of course. He's one of the wealthiest people in town. He bought that antique mansion designed by Frank Lloyd Wright. Everyone in Kankakee has heard the name Stephen Small. But she's certainly never met him. And she doesn't understand what they're talking about.

He's been kidnapped?

And they think she had something to do with it?

The agent sitting at the table points toward the door and says, "Down that hall, there's a room just like this that Danny Edwards is sitting in. Before I came in here, I was talking to him. And when I'm done here, I'm going to go back. We're going to get the story out of one of you. And whoever cooperates is going to get some leniency from the judge."

"You think Danny kidnapped Stephen Small?" Nancy says.

The agent continues, as if he hasn't heard her. "Your boyfriend has a reputation around here. He's a snitch. I'm guessing that it's not going to take long for him to turn on you and try to save his own skin. If I were you, I'd start talking now."

"Can I see Danny?" Nancy asks. "I think we can clear this up if I could just—"

"So you two can get your stories straight? We're not stu-pid, Nancy."

"But you are," the other agent adds, "if you think you can get away with kidnapping a millionaire."

"I'm not trying to get away with anything."

"Why should we believe you, Nancy? You're driving around making ransom calls in the middle of the night—"

"No I'm not."

"—and you're living with a drug dealer."

"He's not a drug dealer. He's cleaned up his act. He's a carpenter now."

"Well, carpenters make a lot less than drug dealers, don't they?" the agent with the glasses says. "Money must be pretty tight right now. That can make people desperate, can't it?"

Nancy opens her mouth to speak but stops herself. She thinks of how strange Danny has been acting, how stressed out he's been.

She wonders if he could have something to do with what the police are talking about. But then she pushes the thought out of her mind. There is no way Danny could be involved in something like this.

Sure, he sold drugs in the past. He isn't perfect.

But kidnapping?

That isn't Danny. He is a good person, deep down.

"I asked you a question," the agent says forcefully.

Nancy snaps back to the present.

"What?" she says. "I'm sorry I didn't hear you."

"Did you or did you not stop at the bait shop in Aroma Park last night and make a phone call?"

"Sure," she says. "Danny made a call. He was calling his—"

"And the night before," the agent says, "where were you at approximately three a.m.? You were making another phone call, weren't you?"

Nancy thinks. She can't keep pace with all that's happening. She remembers picking up Danny at the railroad crossing. She remembers him making a phone call.

But if they think he's mixed up in this, then she doesn't want to get him in any trouble. She wants desperately to talk to him.

I can't tell them anything, she thinks. *Not until I talk to Danny and figure out what's going on.*

"I was home," Nancy says.

"We know you're lying," the agent says with deadly earnestness. "And if you keep lying, the grave you're digging for yourself is only going to get deeper."

CHAPTER 32

September 4
7:00 p.m.

AFTER HOURS OF QUESTIONING—a whole day practically—they lead Nancy out of the room in handcuffs. She is hungry and tired. Her skin is clammy with sweat. She wishes she could go home, take a warm bath, and curl up in bed and sleep for about twelve hours.

Instead, they lead her down a narrow corridor to a series of jail cells. Once she's inside, they have her turn her back toward the bars so they can unlock her handcuffs.

"I want to see my son," she says, rubbing her wrists. "He needs his mother."

The agent with glasses glares at her.

"I'm sure Stephen Small wants to see his sons too," the agent says. "I'm sure his boys need their father."

With that, he turns and leaves. A female police officer in uniform remains standing outside the cell.

Nancy can't imagine why they think they need a guard posted outside her jail cell. She isn't a dangerous criminal. She isn't going to escape. But then she understands why the officer is there. They want someone nearby in case she decides to tell them something important.

She can't imagine what they think she might know.

There is a bed in the room, nothing more than a cot really, and a metal toilet with no seat. The cinder-block walls are painted a drab yellow. The room stinks like its last occupant didn't know what a shower was.

Nancy doesn't particularly want to touch the mattress—who knows who has slept on it?—but it's the only place to sit besides the floor, and she figures that must be even more gross.

She lies down. The thin mattress provides very little comfort. The wire springs press against her back.

She tries to ignore the discomfort and stares at the ceiling, thinking. This is the first opportunity she's had to really let her thoughts catch up with what's been happening. The FBI agents bombarded her with questions for hours. The only time they left her alone, she assumes, was when they were down the hall doing the same to Danny.

She thinks she stuck to her story, but they kept catching her in inconsistencies. She didn't want to tell them about picking Danny up at three o'clock in the morning or about any phone calls he made that night. But at first she told them she was sleeping and later said she was watching a movie.

It doesn't matter, she thinks. *Once they find Stephen Small and all of this gets sorted out, then I'll be free to go.*

She didn't do anything wrong. So this nightmare can't go on much longer. Can it?

She thinks of Danny, wherever he is. He must be scared too. She wishes she could comfort him.

But then she stops herself. It seems more and more clear that he's involved in this mess somehow. His behavior has been so weird lately. There was the box he built in the garage. The way he disappeared for hours in the middle of the night. The strange late-night drive to supposedly get her bike fixed. And the three a.m. pickup at the railroad tracks.

Danny's erratic behavior should have been a telltale sign that he was up to something. The way he snapped at her. The way he almost hit her. The way his mind has seemed a million miles away for the past few days.

Nancy thinks that he must have been roped into being involved. Maybe the drug dealer he used to work for coerced him because Danny still owed him money. Maybe other past associates tricked Danny.

This couldn't be Danny's idea.

But then she remembers him sitting in the kitchen, next to Benji, drawing designs on paper. He wouldn't tell her what he was building. But it had been him who built the strange box in the garage, him who drew the designs, him who went to the lumberyard and bought supplies.

Danny wasn't following anyone's orders, doing anyone else's bidding.

Now Nancy's mind turns to Benji and the memory of him sitting next to Danny, drawing pictures. She'd liked the sight of the two of them together. She remembers thinking that Danny could be a good father figure for Benji.

Could she have been that wrong about him? She has the desperate need to see her son, to hold him in her arms.

When I get out of this mess, she thinks, *I'm going to be the best mother I can possibly be.*

She vows to love him and hold him and stay away from any bad influences.

She'll stay away from men like Danny, she swears to herself.

She suddenly recognizes how stupid she's been, lying to protect Danny. Her concern should be for Benji. She needs to get out of here. She needs to be with her son. Let Danny worry about himself. She needs to worry about her child.

Down the hall from her jail cell, Nancy hears a commotion. Urgent voices. The female officer posted outside her cell glances Nancy's way, then heads down the hall to find out what is happening.

Wait, Nancy thinks. *I'm ready to tell the truth.*

CHAPTER 33

DANNY EDWARDS SITS IN an interrogation room similar to the one Nancy was questioned in. His eyes are bloodshot, with dark circles underneath. He doesn't know how long the questioning has gone on, but they've finally given him a break.

And a cigarette.

He takes a drag. The room is so quiet he can hear the flame eating away at the paper and tobacco. He tilts his head back and exhales a long stream of smoke that puddles against the ceiling, creating a hazy cloud around the yellow fluorescent bulbs.

Danny isn't worried. He hasn't told them anything. He's denied everything. He knows they know he is lying, but he also knows how the police and FBI work. Just because they know he did it doesn't mean they can prove he did it. It doesn't matter if there are inconsistencies in his stories or if they know he's lying.

They have no evidence.

He's worked the police before, and he'll work them again this time. He knows he holds the cards here. He isn't going to tell them anything they need to know—not unless there's something in it for him.

He hears the bolt being pulled back on the other side of the door. The agent who was questioning him earlier, the one with glasses, swings the door open and looks in at Danny.

"The clock is ticking, Danny. What side of this thing do you want to be on?"

Danny stubs the cigarette out on the table. He flicks it into the corner defiantly.

"How many times do I have to tell you?" he says, shaking his head. "I don't know what you're talking about."

The agent steps inside. He leaves the door to the interrogation room hanging open behind him. A uniformed police officer stands behind him, so it's not as if Danny can escape, but still this is something different. Something has changed. They're not coming in for another marathon round of questioning. This is going to be quick.

Maybe Danny doesn't hold all the cards after all.

The FBI agent holds up a police radio and rotates the volume knob so Danny can hear it. Static crackles, and voices talk back and forth.

"...all available units..."

"...Pembroke County..."

"...Mercedes matching the description..."

"...keep the plane in the air until we get officers in the area..."

"...let's try to find it before the sun goes down..."

The agent turns the volume back down, then leans close to Danny's face and says coolly, "An airplane with infrared sensors found Stephen Small's missing Mercedes, Danny. I'm guessing Stephen is stashed somewhere nearby. We're getting closer. If you want any chance of leniency, you better cooperate now."

Danny sits back, takes a deep breath. All day he's been calm, but now his limbs start to tremble.

The agent says, "On the phone, you said Stephen had forty-eight hours of air. We're approaching forty-eight hours, Danny. Kidnapping is a serious charge, but it's not the same as murder. If this thing turns into murder, you're looking at the death penalty."

Danny tries to swallow, his throat suddenly very dry.

He's been wrong all day. He has no cards in his hands. He's only been bluffing. It's time to fold.

"Okay," Danny says. "I'll take you to him."

CHAPTER 34

NANCY STANDS AT THE bars of her cell, trying to look down the hallway. She can't see anything, but she hears commotion. Lots of voices and static from the police radio. She hasn't been able to make out everything, but she understands enough. The police are going somewhere. They think they know where Stephen Small is being kept prisoner.

A knot of people begins walking down the hall toward Nancy's cell. A group of cops and FBI agents are clustered around Danny. He is in handcuffs. His head is hanging low.

"Danny," Nancy says, her voice a whisper full of fear. "What's happening?"

Danny looks up at her.

"I'm sorry, honey," he says. "I didn't mean to hurt anyone."

As he passes by, she stares at him. The yellow lighting makes his skin look pallid, his hair greasy, his eyes red with burst capillaries. More than just his appearance disgusts her. The way he carries himself, as if he doesn't care what's going on, as if all of this is some kind of inconvenience to *him*. His apology to her lacked any sort of conviction in its tone. He's not sorry.

She sees him in a way she's never seen him before.

He's a thug.

A selfish, no-good narcissist who only cares about himself.

A criminal who would rather sell drugs than get a job.

How could she have ever fallen for him?

Tears fill her eyes as Danny and the rest of his entourage disappear down the hall. Nancy turns her head and the woman cop returns and stands outside the jail cell.

There is no sympathy in the woman's face.

"You better hope they find Stephen Small alive," the woman says. "If he's not, you're going to get the electric chair."

"But I didn't know," Nancy says, sobbing.

"They shave your head, you know," the woman says. "So your hair doesn't catch on fire."

Nancy collapses to the floor, weeping. She hears the woman's boots retreat down the hallway, leaving her alone with her tears.

"I want to see my son," she wails.

Her cries echo down the empty hallway.

No one is listening.

CHAPTER 35

"STOP HERE," DANNY SAYS.

The FBI agent driving the car pulls to a stop and puts the vehicle in park. They are in the sand hills outside of Kankakee. The sun is low in the sky, coating the clouds in red and casting a pink, bloody hue onto the sandy ground.

The driver and the agent in the passenger seat get out. The one with the glasses opens the back door of the sedan for Danny, who steps out. His hands are cuffed.

The irony is not lost on Danny that two days ago he was the one leading a handcuffed man down this same path.

This time, instead of just Danny and Stephen Small, Danny is joined by an entire contingent of FBI agents, police, paramedics. There are people all around him, waiting for him to take them to the place where he buried Stephen Small.

"This way," Danny says.

He walks through the sandy soil.

Danny's stomach is knotted, as if someone has taken his intestines and twisted them into a tight ball.

Off to his left, Danny hears a crunch. He pauses and looks over. One of the cops lifts his shoe and looks down. Beneath his foot is a crushed pair of eyeglasses.

The glasses that had fallen off Stephen Small's face.

"Hurry up," one of the agents says, shoving Danny forward.

Danny continues until he spots the PVC pipe sticking out of the ground.

"There," he says.

From the tube sticking out of the ground, it's easy to see the disturbed segment of ground where the rest of the pipe is located, leading to a large swath of disturbed earth.

"He's buried down there," Danny says, then adds, "I gave him food and water."

Officers come in with shovels and get to work. One of the agents leans over the pipe and calls to Stephen Small.

"Mr. Small, it's the police," he shouts. "We're almost there. Just wait a little while longer."

There's no answer.

Danny stands back. His heart hammers in his chest.

He remembers pointing the gun at Stephen Small and the fear he saw on the man's face. Later, when Stephen didn't want to get into the box, Danny had assured him he would live.

Danny had believed his own words.

The cops work furiously, throwing shovelfuls of dirt. Several of them are digging, but the work is slow.

Hurry up, Danny thinks. *Hurry.*

Finally, one of the shovels strikes wood. The officers double their efforts, trying to clear the lid.

"Hang in there, Mr. Small!" one of the agents shouts.

They get enough room around the edge of the box, and an officer kneels and wedges his fingers underneath the lid. He pulls up, and the still partially buried plywood groans under the weight.

Then he pries the lid open so everyone can see inside.

CHAPTER 36

STEPHEN SMALL IS LYING in a curled ball, like a fetus.

He isn't moving.

An EMT kneels down next to him, placing two fingers on his neck, searching for a pulse from the carotid artery. Another EMT leans next to the hole, ready to help.

After only a few seconds, the EMT closest to Stephen looks at the agent in charge and shakes his head.

"He's dead," the EMT says.

Danny's legs go wobbly. He feels like he could throw up. He begins taking deep breaths—long and slow—trying to get himself under control.

Then it occurs to him. What he's doing—breathing deeply—was exactly what Stephen Small couldn't do. Danny had buried a man underground and he had suffocated.

The EMTs step away from the hole, and a new process begins. This is no longer a rescue mission—it is a homicide scene. Detectives begin photographing the body. Others start taping off the perimeter.

The agent in charge approaches Danny. He's furious. Danny can tell by looking at him. But there's something else in his expression too. Sadness. They've solved the crime, but it's too late. There's no satisfaction in the resolution, only anger and sorrow and confusion about why this had to happen at all.

The agent takes Danny by the arm and leads him close to the grave.

"Take a good look," the agent says. "I want you to see what you've done."

Stephen Small's skin is gray. His milky eyes are vacant, staring at nothing. His loafers are in the corner of the box, and his bare feet are contorted with the toes curled up. Up until this moment, Danny had thought perhaps the EMTs were wrong. He had thought there was still a chance that Stephen Small might sit up, yawn, and look around with sleepy eyes.

But seeing the body this close, there is no mistaking it. A dead man looks different from someone who's sleeping. There is no air inflating his lungs. There is no blood pulsing through his veins.

Stephen Small is not asleep.

The man Danny kidnapped is gone forever.

Another officer approaches them, holding up a length of PVC pipe.

"This diameter is way too narrow for how long it is," the agent says to his colleague. "There was no way for him to expel his carbon dioxide out of the box. And no way to pull in adequate oxygen from the outside. We'll have to wait on the autopsy, but judging by the rigor mortis, I'd say he's been dead for at least a day. I doubt he survived more than a few hours with this ridiculous contraption."

The agent looks at Danny. "He might have been dead before you ever made the first phone call to request a ransom."

With that, the agent walks away, getting back to work.

"What made you think he had forty-eight hours of air?" the agent in charge asks Danny.

Danny stares at the body of Stephen Small.

"I don't know what I was thinking," Danny says, and it seems to him that it's a blanket statement that could describe the ill-conceived air pipe as well as the whole kidnapping scheme. It is a statement that might encompass his entire life, practically every decision he has ever made.

I don't know what I was thinking.

"How does it feel to be a murderer?" the agent asks Danny.

"I never meant to kill him," Danny says. "I'm no murderer."

"Even now," the agent says, gesturing to the body, "you're unwilling to take responsibility for your actions. Unbelievable. You, Danny Edwards, are the most reprehensible human I've ever met."

Danny doesn't argue.

"You *and* your accomplice," the agent adds.

"Accomplice?" Danny says.

CHAPTER 37

NANCY IS BACK IN the interrogation room.

It's late at night. Earlier today, she told the female police officer that she needed to talk to someone, but hours passed before the woman led her down the hall, back to the interrogation room.

The agent in charge is already there, waiting.

His tie and suit jacket are gone, and his collar, now open, has yellowed with sweat and dust. His hair is disheveled, and his eyes have dark crescent moons beneath them. Despite how exhausted he obviously is, his expression is as alert as when she first spoke to him.

"I'm ready to tell you everything I know," Nancy says. "I didn't do anything and I didn't know what Danny was up to."

The agent gives her a look that silences her.

"We found Stephen Small," he says.

"Good," she says. "Thank God."

"He's dead."

"Oh no," she says. "That's awful."

"When you and Danny concocted this scheme, whose idea was it?"

Nancy stares at him, dumbfounded.

"I told you," she says. "I had no—"

"Yeah, yeah," the agent says. "You just happened to go for a ride with Danny late at night to get your bicycle fixed. And then he called the guy and it turned out he couldn't fix the bike after all. You expect us to believe that?"

"It's the truth," she says, and then clarifies, "That's what Danny told me anyway."

The agent leans in and puts his elbows on the table. His glasses have gotten progressively dirtier as the day has gone on, and he stares at her through smudged lenses.

"Okay," he says. "Let's talk about the truth. Danny told us that you picked him up after he buried Stephen Small alive."

Nancy goes cold.

"That's true," she says quietly.

"So you knew he was burying Stephen Small out in the sand hills?"

"No!" she says, practically yelling. "I picked him up. I didn't know what he was doing."

The agent smirks and shakes his head disapprovingly.

Nancy knows how ridiculous it sounds. She picked Danny up late at night in the middle of nowhere, and the agent is supposed to believe she didn't know what she was doing there. She can hardly believe it herself. What was she thinking trusting Danny?

"You told us before that you were sleeping. Oh, wait." He consults his notes. "You told us you were watching a video. Oh, wait, you told us both lies."

"I'm sorry," she says, flustered, unsure what more to say.

"Which is it?" the agent says. "Were you sleeping? Watching a video? Or helping your drug-dealing boyfriend commit felony kidnapping?"

"No," Nancy blurts out. "None of those."

"So what's your story now?"

Nancy takes a deep breath.

"I picked Danny up," she says. "I didn't know what he was doing. I didn't want to know. If I had any idea he was kidnapping someone, I never would have gone along. I would have run as far away from him as I could."

"Lady," the agent says, "you should have gotten as far away from him as you could a long time ago. But you didn't. You knew he was a drug dealer and you stayed with him. Why would I believe you didn't know about this?"

The agent rises and clears his throat.

"Nancy Rish, you are under arrest for the kidnapping and murder of Stephen Small. You have the right to remain silent—"

"No," Nancy says, tears spilling down her cheeks. "I didn't do anything."

"Yes, you did," the agent says. "You helped Danny Edwards kidnap and murder Stephen Small."

He continues reciting the Miranda rights, but Nancy doesn't hear him. She's too preoccupied crying. She puts her head in her hands and sobs.

She can think of only one thing.

Her son growing up without a mother.

CHAPTER 38

10 years later

NANCY SITS IN THE visitation area of the Logan Correctional Center. Around her, other women, all wearing the same prison-issued jumpsuits, wait for their family members. Husbands enter and hug their wives. Sons and daughters come in and either embrace their mothers or sit down in a huff, glaring at the women.

Nancy knows some of the women. Others are just faces in the halls of the prison. Some of them are nice; others are mean. Some are tough and scary, and others cry at night, weeping for what they've lost.

Nancy keeps craning her head toward the entrance. She is especially anxious today. She always expects him to look younger than he is, as if time will have stopped on the outside world while she's been locked away. She expects an eight-year-old boy to run and leap into her arms like she's just been away for the weekend. But then the real Benji strides in—a man now, no longer a boy—wearing a button-down shirt and tie. Today, he holds a black square object in his hand and grins sheepishly.

Nancy's mouth bursts into a wide, uncontrollable smile. Tears pool in her eyes.

"I did it, Mom," Ben says, holding out the object.

It's the cap from his graduation regalia, complete with a yellow tassel marked with the words *Class of '97*.

She throws her arms around his neck and grips him in a tight hug.

"I'm proud of you," she says, unable to keep herself from crying. "I wish I could have been there."

"Me too," he says, and begins to cry too.

A guard walks toward their table and tells them to separate. Wiping her eyes, Nancy sits. Ben does too. She wants to hold his hand, but that is against the rules also. It's hard to sit this close to him and not touch him, but she'll try to sneak another hug before he leaves.

Ben tells her about the graduation ceremony, which fills her with joy and sadness. She wants to hear all about it, but hearing him speak of the ceremony—a milestone event in his life that she couldn't be there for—is also like pressing on a bruise that never heals.

She's been locked up for ten years, and still the frustration over her powerlessness never ebbs, never weakens. She can't be there for her son and can't imagine a more painful way to live her day-to-day life.

Inevitably, as it does every time Ben visits, their conversation turns to the status of her appeals. Her lawyer is getting ready to file the papers, she says.

Nancy was sentenced to life in prison for murder, with another thirty years tacked on for aggravated kidnapping. In short, she is supposed to spend the rest of her life behind bars, without the possibility of parole. If she can't overturn her conviction, she will die in prison of old age.

It could have been worse. Because the murder was committed during the act of a felony, the crime qualified for the death penalty. That's the sentence Danny Edwards received.

There is a rumor going around that the state plans to abolish the death penalty, which would commute Danny's sentence to life in prison without parole, essentially the same as Nancy's.

But Nancy is confident that her appeal will overturn her conviction.

It has to. She's already missed her son's childhood. She doesn't want to miss the rest of his life.

"I promise you," Nancy says, reaching out and breaking the rules by grabbing his hand, "I will spend however long it takes to get out of here. I will come home to you."

Ben takes this cue to hug her. When a security guard heads their way, they split up and Ben heads for the door, holding his graduation cap at his side.

Tears streak Nancy's cheeks.

As she heads back to her cell, she thinks about what landed her here. Not the murder of Stephen Small, but what she is actually guilty of—blindly loving the wrong man.

She thinks about Danny and wonders where he is. She

imagines him sitting in a cell, thinking somehow that he is a victim in all this. It wasn't fair he couldn't make ends meet. It wasn't fair other people had so much money. It wasn't fair that Stephen Small died from asphyxiation when Danny never actually wanted to hurt him. Danny always blamed everyone else.

She wonders if Danny feels any guilt for the lives he destroyed. Not just those of Stephen Small and his family.

But her life too.

She settles back into her cell and sits down on the bunk. Her cell is similar to the first one she was locked in all those years ago: metal toilet, metal sink, cinder-block walls. It makes her long for the leaking dishwasher and chipped paint of her old town house.

The cell also has a small desk in the corner, and taped above it are pictures that Ben has sent her over the years. She missed his first day of middle school, his first day of high school. She wasn't there for him when he was getting ready for prom. She didn't help him study for his SATs. She won't be there to see him off to college.

So much has been taken from her.

It isn't fair, she thinks.

Then she stops herself and wonders for a moment if she is just like Danny, putting all the blame on someone else.

She knew Danny was up to something. She didn't know it was kidnapping. She didn't know it was murder. But she knew something bad was happening, and she went along with it. She wasn't just ignorant of what happened. She *chose* ignorance despite warning sign after warning sign.

A man died.

A wife lost her husband.

Three boys lost their father.

Could she have stopped this from happening if she'd done anything differently? Could she have at least protected herself and her son by getting as far away from Danny as possible?

What could she have done differently?

She lies down on her bunk and stares at the ceiling, thinking.

She won't come to any answers today, nor anytime soon. As she looks around her prison cell, she knows there will be plenty of time to ponder these questions.

Finally honest with herself, Nancy Rish knows she will be in prison for a long, long time.

MURDER IN PARADISE

JAMES PATTERSON

with **CHRISTOPHER CHARLES**

PROLOGUE

1990

A FLASH OF COLOR broke in on her dream and startled her awake.

I knew I shouldn't have had that second Vodka Collins, Bonnie thought.

Hard alcohol always made her jumpy, restless. She rolled onto her side, shut her eyes, felt a faint mountain breeze coming through the cracked window.

But then she heard what sounded like a man clearing his throat, and she knew it was this sound, and not her dream, that had woken her. The noise hadn't come from the man lying beside her, who wasn't so much asleep as passed out, but from somewhere farther off in the room. She sat up, reached for the lamp on her nightstand.

"Don't bother," the intruder said. "This will be over real quick."

Bonnie's first instinct was to pull the covers up around her neck. She looked toward the voice and squinted. A large silhouette emerged from the darkness. She couldn't be sure, but she thought the man was smiling. Maybe this was a joke. Another prank being played by one of the patrons from the bar.

"I don't know you are, but this isn't funny," Bonnie said. "In fact, it's criminal. If you're still here by the time I switch this light on, I will press charges."

Her own words sounded strange to her, like she'd borrowed the phrasing from her schoolmarm mother. Maybe, she thought, that's how people cope with terror: by channeling someone else.

"He don't wake easy," the intruder said, gesturing to the other side of the bed with what Bonnie now saw was a long-barreled revolver. "Must be all that Jack D," he added.

So he had been watching them at the bar. Another local who didn't want an Orange County developer— especially a female developer—scooping up property on *their* mountain. She would just have to show them that she was here to stay, that she hadn't bought Camp Nelson Lodge on a whim: she'd fallen in love with the place. She sat up straighter, reached for the light. The porcelain base of the lamp seemed to explode before she heard the shot. She screamed, slammed her back flat against the wall.

The man beside her stirred, then came fully awake. He threw the covers back, swung his legs out of bed, and stumbled forward, still drunk. A second shot and he staggered, grabbed the dresser, brought it down on top of him.

The room went silent just long enough for Bonnie to realize she was going to die. Somehow the setting felt all wrong. Or rather the setting was right, but the timing was wrong. She was supposed to finish raising her kids here. Grow old here. Spend her waning years sharing the backwoods with her grandchildren.

She tried to call for help but couldn't find the air inside her. The man raised his gun. Bonnie shut her eyes.

It was over.

CHAPTER 1

1989

"WE DROVE FIVE HOURS and he's the one who's late?" Jim said.

"By five minutes," Bonnie said. "Besides, the drive along that gorge was as beautiful as anything I've ever seen."

"Made me carsick."

Bonnie climbed atop the picnic table and turned in a slow circle, craning her neck to see the tops of the sequoias, taking deep breaths of mountain air. Jim sat on the bench, brushed a pine needle from the flannel shirt he'd worn to blend in with the locals.

"I feel like the Marlboro Man," he said.

Bonnie didn't hear him, or at least pretended not to. Jim scanned the property. With its stone façade, the lodge appeared sturdy enough, but the two-story motel looming in the background looked like it might topple from one well-placed kick, and the small cabins, set at random distances along the periphery of the main clearing, were bordering on disrepair. Nestled among the world's tallest trees, with the Sierra Nevada rising to the east, it was, as Bonnie said, a beautiful spot. But there were a lot of beautiful places in the world, and Jim didn't see the point in anchoring yourself to just one.

"That must be Rudy," Bonnie said, nodding at the short, squat man exiting the main building.

"About time," Jim said.

"Shush now," Bonnie told him.

Rudy waved as he walked toward them. Jim stood, looked at his watch.

"Mr. and Mrs. Hood?" Rudy called.

Bonnie nodded.

"Welcome to Camp Nelson Lodge. I'm really sorry about the wait. The plumbing in the lodge got cranky. I'm not going to lie: that happens pretty regular these days."

Bonnie shook his hand, then turned to Jim: "You see? I told you we're blessed to have a realtor who doesn't work Sundays. We're going to get the inside story."

Now that Rudy was up close, Jim noticed a fresh grease stain running across the man's ratty polo shirt. Rudy had muscular forearms, a barrel chest, and a gut that suggested long nights in the saloon. His salt-and-pepper hair was in bad need of a shampooing. Jim pegged him as a ne'er-do-well: a middle-aged man who'd attached himself to a near-vacant lodge in order to keep a roof over his own lazy head.

"What exactly do you do here again?" Jim asked.

"I'm the caretaker."

Jim glanced around.

"No offense," he said, "but it doesn't look like you've been busy."

Bonnie gave him a sharp jab with her elbow.

"It's okay," Rudy said. "More honesty: I'm a staff of one with no budget. I've been hoping someone would come along and sink some money into this place."

"Sink?" Jim asked.

Rudy grinned.

"I mean invest," he said. "Look around. There isn't another parcel of land like this one anywhere in the world. Every morning I step outside and I remember that life is a miracle. If I had kids, I'd raise 'em right here."

"Maybe you *should* have been a realtor," Jim said.

"Nah," Rudy said. "I'm not trying to sell you anything. Truth is, it's sad what's happened to Camp Nelson Lodge. It used to be bustling with city folks whose souls needed a rest. They'd show up looking like they'd been wound so tight their nerves were snapping, and within a couple of days you'd see all that tension just leave their bodies. This place can be magic that way. But now it's just part of the Edwards Group's portfolio, and they've let it rot. We haven't taken a guest in two years. The saloon is still open for locals, but that's it. Like I said, I've been praying Edwards'd sell. I'd buy the place myself if I had the money."

"I used to come here with my parents when I was a kid," Bonnie said. "I never stopped dreaming about the sequoias. You're right: Camp Nelson is magical."

Rudy gave a solemn nod; Jim sniggered.

"I'd settle for functional," Jim said.

* * *

Rudy took them on a tour, beginning with the lodge. The lobby was a long, open space with twin stone fireplaces, one at either end. The ceiling beams were made of solid logs ("This is a logging community," Rudy pointed out), and the floor of ceramic tile. The walls were covered with unfinished wood panels, which Jim thought gave an otherwise stately room the look of a semifinished basement.

"It's real wood, Jim," Bonnie said, "not laminate."

The dining room/meeting hall featured wraparound windows and looked onto a small meadow separated from the forest by a stream.

"The view's not bad—I'll give you that. But even my grandmother wouldn't have put up with this wallpaper," Jim said.

"You can change the wallpaper," Bonnie said. "The view is for keeps."

Jim rapped on one of the windows with his knuckle.

"You'll have to change these, too, if you plan to be open for ski season," he said.

Rudy seemed amused by their back and forth. He led them out the back door and on to the motel. With its wooden shingles and log pillars it looked exactly like the saloon-hotel combo from countless Western flicks. There were signs of termites on the porch, and the foyer smelled of mold. The doors to the large but utterly bare rooms all hung open.

"Nothing for folks to steal," Rudy said. "Might as well air the place out."

Jim started to say something, then stopped when he noticed his wife smiling like a little girl on a trampoline.

"I have such incredible memories of this place," she said, then turned and ran up the stairs.

Jim and Rudy followed. They found her standing on a rickety balcony, staring out at a large, overgrown meadow.

"They used to stage Civil War reenactments there," she said. "Afterwards, there'd be a Southern-themed buffet."

"I hope you'll let that tradition lie," Jim said.

Rudy chuckled. Once again, Bonnie didn't seem to hear.

CHAPTER 2

RUDY WALKED THEM THROUGH the cabins, which were more like the skeletons of cabins, and then on to the bar: a standalone log structure situated on the access road to the resort. There was an unpaved parking area out front. Jim pointed to crisscrossing, single-tire tracks.

"Bikers?" he asked.

Rudy rolled his eyes.

"Harleys are the loggers' vehicle of choice up here," he said. "No gangs, though, if that's what you're worried about. But I won't lie: it's noisy at closing time."

He dug out his keys and led them inside. It was more saloon than bar, with swinging half-doors, sawdust covering the floor, and nothing hanging on the walls save a silver-framed mirror above the shelves of whiskey. The wooden tables and hardback chairs seemed, like the cabins, to be arranged in no particular order.

"This place turns a profit?" Jim asked.

"There's a small crowd most nights—bigger on weekends. The Edwards Group isn't getting rich off it, but I'd guess they're breaking even. They'd have cut bait before now if they weren't."

Bonnie walked up to the bar, ran her fingers along the zinc.

"This is vintage," she said. "Real mahogany. With a little polish and elbow grease, it might be worth something."

"A diamond in the rough," Rudy said.

He smiled. Bonnie smiled back. The exchange bothered Jim: it was like watching adolescents bond over some pop band he'd never heard of.

"So what do you think?" Rudy asked when they were back outside.

"You know what I think," Bonnie said, still smiling.

"We'll get back to you," Jim told him.

* * *

"I've been developing other people's properties for upwards of twenty years," Bonnie said. "I want a project of my own."

They'd left Rudy and were following the Camp Nelson Trail through a forest of giant Sequoias and mountain streams. Despite the mild temperature and perfect blue sky, they had the trail all to themselves.

"Okay, but why *this* project?" Jim asked.

"Why? Just look at these mountains, Jim."

"Just look at that property. One well-placed kick and half those buildings would fall right over."

"We came here every summer when I was a kid. You know that."

"So you're nostalgic?"

"Look, I know the lodge has been in decline for years, but you couldn't ask for better bones. Just imagine what this place *could* be. Hiking, horseback riding, swimming, fishing—it's all right here. We'll replace those old, rickety mattresses with waterbeds, give each cabin a private sauna. And we'll bring that god-awful bar into the twentieth century."

"The locals seem to like that god-awful bar. You heard your caretaker friend: it's the only thing keeping the place afloat."

"They'll learn to like the new one, too. Just think what a day could be like up here. Think about breakfast at altitude. Stacks of homemade pancakes and fresh fruit and those venison sausages you like. And after breakfast, a nice stroll into the mountains while the air is still cool and the deer are active."

"I'd rather sleep in and go for brunch. You know, there's something to be said for museums and concert halls."

Bonnie stopped midstride, gave him a pointed look.

"Really? How many symphonies have you seen in the last year?"

"I'm thinking about our kids."

"So am I. I don't want them to grow up all urban and neurotic, like me."

"They're only halfway through the school year."

"So they'll finish it out. I'll stay up here, get the place ready. We can talk on the phone every night. You guys'll visit on weekends. That way they get a slow introduction to the place. Think about it. It's a dream life."

They came to a small footbridge, paused to look at the stream below, then stood facing each other, leaning against opposite railings.

"We've got two healthy kids and all the money we could ever spend," Jim said. "I thought we were living our dream life."

"Maybe *you* were."

"What does that mean?"

"This place is the first thing I've asked for—the first thing I've really wanted in all the time we've been married. You, on the other hand—you get everything your heart desires and I never say boo about it."

"Like what?"

"How about that little trip to Spain with your buddies so you could run with the bulls on your forty-fifth birthday? Without me, of course."

"I was gone a week."

"Okay. What about your little trek through the Amazon? Also no wives allowed."

"Again, that was two weeks, not the rest of our lives."

Bonnie rolled her eyes, sucked in a deep breath.

"The point is you needed those trips to get through your midlife crisis, or whatever it was. And I let you have them. Well, I need this. I'm not saying you have to give up the place in Newport, but I *need* this. Our marriage needs this."

Jim started to object, then stopped himself. He bent down, picked up a rock, turned it over in his palm like a prospector appraising the soil.

"I guess it's settled then," he said.

CHAPTER

1990

BONNIE SAT FLIPPING THROUGH a wildflower guide on a brand-new porch swing outside the Camp Nelson Lodge, glancing up anxiously at the road. It was only five days since she last saw her husband and children, but it felt longer. It felt like they belonged to another life, maybe another lifetime—back when she drove a Lexus instead of a Jeep, back when all she could see from her porch was a cluster of suburban mansions and lawns decorated with hydrangeas and plastic flamingos. She didn't miss her lawn, didn't miss anything at all about the 'burbs. It may have taken her forty-seven years, but she'd finally landed where she was meant to be.

She spotted Jim's Mercedes, tossed aside her book, and ran to greet her children. Jim Jr., who'd just turned thirteen, was asleep in the front passenger seat, his mouth hanging open. He'd never in his short life been able to stay awake in a moving vehicle, and Bonnie was already worried about the prospect of him one day getting his license.

The car pulled closer, and she saw eleven-year-old Mindy in the back seat, too engrossed in her *Illustrated Mythology* to look up. Bonnie knew this was a snapshot of the last five hours in her family's life: Jim listening to talk radio, making snarky comments about the hosts and callers; Jim Jr. snoring away with his head slouched against the window; Mindy quietly reading, tracing the pictures with her fingers. It was like Bonnie might as well have made the trip with them.

Jim was the first out of the car.

"You're looking a little crunchier every week," he said, referring to her leather hiking boots, her long ponytail, the beaded necklace he'd never seen her wear before.

"Nice to see you, too," she said, giving him a peck on the cheek. "Maybe you'd better wake up Rumpelstiltskin."

Jim banged on the hood of the car with an open palm.

"Hey, buddy, come on now," he called.

Jim Jr. raised his head, looked around, seemed to want to retreat back into his dream. Mindy ran up and grabbed her mother around the waist.

"It's so beautiful here, Mommy," she said.

"There's my girl," Bonnie said, giving her daughter a squeeze. "God, I missed you."

And Bonnie realized that this was true. She'd had her hands full looking after the guests, renovating the final cabin, supervising the bar, fitting in the occasional hike— but beneath all of that there had been an ache. The nightly phone calls weren't cutting it: she wanted her children there with her. *Soon enough*, she thought. Only a few months left in the school year.

She leaned into the backseat, the smell of bubblegum momentarily replacing the smell of pine, and pulled out Mindy's duffel bag. When she turned around, Rudy was standing there. He reached for the bag, and she felt his hand on hers, felt it linger there a beat too long. Bonnie spun her head, found Jim lifting luggage from the trunk. Oblivious.

* * *

Once the family had unpacked and settled in, they gathered in the dining room around two extra-large ice cream sundaes.

"So what do you kids think?" Bonnie asked. "Maybe some kayaking later? Or a hike?"

Jim cut in before they could answer.

"I'm anxious to baptize that new in-ground pool," he said.

"You hate swimming," Bonnie said.

"Yeah, but I like sitting in a lounge chair with a gin and tonic in my hand."

"Swimming!" Mindy said. "I want to go swimming."

Jim Jr. nodded enthusiastically.

"All right," Bonnie shrugged. "Swimming it is."

She shot her husband a pointed look. She was sure he'd prepped them. For Bonnie, the pool was the least interesting part of the property—the only part you could find back in "civilization," as Jim called it. She'd only had one installed because it seemed to be something guests expected.

The door to the dining area opened and Rudy appeared. Jim watched him walk up to the table. He'd cleaned himself up since that day he first showed them around. Instead of a grease-stained polo shirt he wore a plaid button-down with short sleeves that showed off his bulging forearms. He was younger than Jim originally thought, too—maybe thirty-five or thirty-six? A good ten years younger than Bonnie, but still Jim wondered if he should worry.

"Excuse me," Rudy said. "Sorry to interrupt. I just wanted to bring you the mail before I run my errands in town."

She can't get her own mail? Jim thought.

Bonnie took the small pile, and Rudy left. Her eyes were drawn to a pale-blue envelope addressed in a shaky cursive. The kids started squabbling about whether or not Jim Jr. had spotted a black bear during the drive up ("So you can see in your sleep?" Mindy asked), and Jim took the opportunity to attack the remains of their sundae. Bonnie set aside the flyers and bills, slit the envelope open. Inside, she found a brief note written in block letters on a sheet of matching blue paper:

GO HOME WHILE YOU STILL CAN, YOU RICH BITCH.

She smiled to keep herself from shuddering, then folded the paper in thirds and slid it back inside the envelope.

CHAPTER 4

THAT NIGHT, BONNIE AND Jim stayed in one of the newly updated cabins. Bonnie had set it up with a vase of wildflowers, a chilled bottle of white wine, a hand-stitched duvet. They sat out back in the hot tub, looking up at the stars.

"This isn't so bad," Jim said.

He slid closer to her, put an arm around her shoulders, kissed her neck. Bonnie didn't move a muscle. She didn't seem to know that he was there.

"Goddamn it, Bonnie," Jim said, "what's the matter with you?"

"What do you mean?"

"The cabin, the wine, the hot tub—wasn't that all your idea?"

"I'm sorry, Jim," she said. "It's just...I've got a lot on my mind."

"I thought you came out here to clear your mind. Get away from the stress."

She frowned.

"Maybe not in the first year, Jim. There's a ton to do. To be honest, the place is taking off faster than I thought possible. Any chance we've got the cash flow to build two more cabins?"

It was true that she'd already found herself turning people away, but the suggestion that they expand was a whim. She'd figured out years ago that the best way to distract Jim was to give him what he most enjoyed: the power to say no.

And she needed to distract him. She had no intention of sharing what was really on her mind: another anonymous death threat on pale-blue stationery. Jim would insist at once that it was time to come home, give up this experiment in the woods. Only, as far as Bonnie was concerned, this was home—hers and her children's—and she was prepared to fight for it if need be.

"I don't know," Jim said. "I've got a lot of irons in the fire right now. Our money is spread pretty thin. Maybe in the fall?"

Not an outright no, but Bonnie knew why: Jim was feeling randy. Once again, the world boiled down to what he wanted. It made her so furious that she forgot about the letter for a minute.

"You're so obvious," she said.

"Obvious?"

"You're like a teenage boy."

"Excuse me for wanting a little affection from my wife."

"Affection?"

"Is that so hard to believe?" Jim asked. "I miss you. I miss our life. A year ago we were the glamour couple. The real estate queen and king of SoCal. Now I feel like I'm second fiddle. Maybe not even second."

Bonnie took a long sip of wine.

"That's the problem, Jim: you think of me as your queen. An extension of the business, with side benefits. It's like I'm one-stop shopping. Maybe I just got tired of being convenient."

Jim sat up straighter, was on the verge of saying *Well, there's nothing convenient about you now* when Rudy came bolting around a corner of the cabin.

"Jesus," Jim said. "You might want to put up some fences."

"Sorry," Rudy said. "I tried knocking, but no one answered."

"I wonder why," Jim said.

"What is it?" Bonnie asked.

"There's trouble at the bar. Some of the customers are asking for you."

"Splendid," Bonnie said. "Exactly how I hoped this evening would go."

She reached for a towel, wrapped it around her torso as she stood.

"Tell them I'll be there as soon as I can," she said.

"You mind if I finish your glass?" Jim asked.

CHAPTER 5

ON A SATURDAY NIGHT, Bonnie found the Camp Nelson Saloon, the only watering hole for thirty miles, crowded with locals from every corner of the county. Most of the patrons seemed to be having a good time, laughing, drinking, smoking, bopping to the country music on the jukebox, playing cards or backgammon at the tables. But a cluster of bikers at the bar, their voices drowned out by the general din, appeared to be giving the bartender a hard time.

Rudy greeted Bonnie at the door.

"Thanks for coming," he said. "They wouldn't take no for an answer."

"What was the question?" Bonnie asked.

"Hey, there she is," one of the bikers yelled, waving her over with a gesture that looked like a command. He was well over six feet, ruddy faced, wore a heavily patched denim vest and a red bandana. Bonnie started forward, took her time crossing the floor. Rudy followed close behind.

"What seems to be the problem?" Bonnie asked.

She counted five of them altogether. They hopped off their stools, formed a semicircle around her and Rudy.

"I was hoping you could tell us," the one who'd called her over said. "Did we offend you somehow?"

"I don't understand," Bonnie said.

"Seems the prices have been raised, but only on what we like to drink."

"You mean the draft beers?" Bonnie asked.

"Yeah, that's exactly what I mean."

Bonnie knew this was coming. In fact, she'd hoped it was coming. The man wasn't wrong: she wanted him and his entourage gone. They were rowdy, coarse. Their motorcycles disturbed her guests. They disturbed *her*.

"I'm sorry," she said, "but the distributor raised his prices. I had no choice."

"He gouges you, so you gouge us. Is that it?"

"It's business," Rudy said. "You'd have done the same."

"Don't tell me what I would've done."

The bikers surrounding them folded their arms, shifted their weight back and forth. Bonnie sensed a wrong turn coming.

"Look," she said, "I'm sorry for the inconvenience. How about a pitcher on the house?"

"How about you keep the prices where they were?"

"Sorry, can't do it," Bonnie said.

To her dismay, she realized she was guilty of the very complaint she'd just leveled against Jim: she had the power to say no, and she was enjoying it.

"Well, then you and your little houseboy are in for a tough time."

Rudy stepped forward; Bonnie put a hand on his chest.

"If you can't be civil, then you need to leave now," she told the man.

He grinned.

"Sorry, you prissy skank," he said, "but we were here first."

He reached behind him, took his drink from the bar, held it out toward Bonnie, then slowly and deliberately let go. The glass exploded at her feet. Beer soaked her sneakers and jeans. She jumped back just as Rudy sprung forward. The whole bar was watching now. Before Bonnie could register what was happening, Rudy had the man's arm up behind his back and was running him outside. The entourage followed on their heels.

Kelly, the tall and emaciated bartender who'd come with the place, handed her new boss a rag while making only the slightest attempt to hide her smirk. *Well*, Bonnie thought, *it's clear whose side you're on.*

Rudy came back. His hair was disheveled but he appeared otherwise unscathed.

"Are you all right?" Bonnie asked.

Rudy nodded. They heard the bikes firing up in the lot.

"I wouldn't count on this being over, though," he said.

He put a hand on her shoulder. She was about to take it when she noticed that all eyes remained fixed on her. She cupped her hands around her mouth, shouted: "Next round is on the house."

* * *

"I'm telling you, it was nothing," Bonnie said. "A simple misunderstanding."

They were lying in bed under the skylight with a fire winding down across the room.

"Really?" Jim said. "Because you came back drenched in beer and looking white as a sheet."

He seemed genuinely worried, and Bonnie felt a pang of guilt as she realized she didn't even want that much from him anymore.

"I promise, it's all fine," she said. "But now I really need to get some sleep."

She rolled onto her side, fought back a gasp when she spotted what looked like a male figure watching them through a part in the curtains. She leapt out of bed, started for the window, watched the figure dart off.

"What is it?" Jim asked.

"Just shutting the curtain," she said.

CHAPTER 6

BONNIE ROSE EARLY, FIXED a three-course breakfast for Jim and the kids.

"It's French themed," she announced. "French toast, French roast, and—just to make sure you get enough carbs—French croissants."

"I could really use that coffee," Jim said. "I guess I'm not used to wine at altitude."

"Help yourself," Bonnie said.

She'd hoped for a picnic in the meadow, but the sky was overcast, so they sat in the dining room of what Rudy called the proprietor's apartment: a five-room home set off in the main lodge. The kids were still in their pajamas, still blinking sleep from their eyes. Bonnie watched them lick syrup off their forks and felt as though she were watching a memory—the memory that would carry her through their long, five-day absence. Just a few more months to go, she reminded herself. Seventy-two days, to be exact, before they'd be living here instead of visiting.

After breakfast, Jim Jr. insisted on a round of Uno.

"Why don't you kids get washed up and changed first?" Bonnie said. "I'll meet you in the living room."

Jim helped her clear the table, then said he was going out to grab some air.

"I've got a long drive ahead of me," he said. "And I'm feeling a little fuzzy."

"Better hurry," Bonnie told him. "It's going to start thundering any minute."

An hour later, Bonnie and the children were sitting on the living room floor, arguing over whether Mindy had remembered to say Uno before her last discard, when Jim came rushing in, yelling Bonnie's name.

"What is it?" Bonnie asked.

"You need to come see this," he said. "Now. Kids, you stay here."

She followed him through the lodge, asking again and again what was wrong. But as soon as they stepped outside, she saw. The windshield on her Jeep was smashed to bits. Someone had pegged it dead-center with an object large enough and hard enough to suck the whole sheet of glass inward.

"My god," she said. "Who the hell..."

"It must have happened while I was out walking," Jim said.

Bonnie stood at the edge of the porch, staring, her arms akimbo, her mouth wide open. She figured the fear would come later, once Jim was gone. Right now, she wanted to kill someone. Starting with that biker at the bar.

Jim walked over to the Jeep, opened the driver-side door, and pulled out a red brick wrapped in a pale-blue sheet of paper.

"Let me see that," Bonnie said, running up to him. He handed it over without objecting. Bonnie tore off the rubber bands, let the brick drop to the ground as she straightened out the note.

It read: LAST WARNING, YOU RICH BITCH.

* * *

The thunder was short lived, though the rain lasted into the late afternoon. They sat by the bay window in the dining room and watched the storm while they played Chutes and Ladders, Monopoly, Go Fish. Jim was quiet and on edge, would snap at the children when they broke the rules or asked for a do-over. Bonnie chatted nonstop, laughed when nothing was funny, praised the kids for nothing in particular.

"Are you guys fighting?" Mindy asked.

"You're not supposed to ask that, stupid," her brother scolded.

"Hey, don't talk to your sister like that," Jim said.

"I think we all need snacks," Bonnie said. "I'll go heat up some cookies."

"And I'll help," Jim said.

Bonnie should have anticipated that: the last thing she wanted right now was to be alone with Jim. In the kitchen, out of earshot of the children, he launched right in.

"*Last warning?*" he quoted. "You want to tell me how many others there have been?"

"None that came with property damage."

"That doesn't answer my question."

"No, it doesn't," she said, transferring a batch of snickerdoodles from tin to tray. "You told me you don't want to be involved in lodge business. Well, this is lodge business."

"No," Jim corrected her, "business is ledgers and balance sheets. This is a death threat."

Bonnie slid the tray into the oven and set the timer for five minutes.

"Stop being so dramatic," she said. "They're just trying to scare me off. If they wanted to hurt me, I'd be hurt."

"*They?* So you know who's behind this?"

"I have an idea. No proof."

"Then why won't you go to the police?"

"You know, if you're really going to pretend to help me, you could at least pour the milk."

"Answer my question."

"I told you, I'll call once the kids are gone. I don't want to frighten them. I don't want them to be afraid of this place. And don't you say anything to them, either."

Jim punched the counter with the side of his fist.

"Fine," he said. "I'll fill them in at your funeral."

"Just pour the damn milk," Bonnie said.

* * *

The rain let up around four p.m., then stopped altogether. Bonnie hid the Jeep before seeing Jim and the kids off. Mindy cried, clutched her mother's leg, begged to stay.

"Soon, love," Bonnie said.

"I bet that makes you happy," Jim said under his breath.

Bonnie brushed him off, leaned into the car and gave Jim Jr. a kiss.

"Sleep well," she said.

* * *

That night, Bonnie sat at her desk in her office while Rudy paced the room. She unlocked a drawer, slid it open, pulled out a folder containing a half-dozen pale-blue sheets of paper. She placed the first threatening letter side-by-side with the one Jim had taken from her car.

"The writing is the same," she said.

"Of course it's the same," Rudy said. "I'm begging you to let me handle those rednecks."

Bonnie raised one eyebrow.

"You want me to sanction violence?" she asked.

"You tried the cops. They're not going to do anything until you're dead."

"That's not exactly what they said. They need proof."

"Yeah, well... I don't."

Bonnie slid both letters back into the file.

"Calm the testosterone," she said. "Why don't we try setting up some cameras first?"

Rudy grinned, walked around behind the desk, began massaging her shoulders.

"I'm worried about you," he said. "These guys run around in the dark like cowards. They are cowards. But cowards can be the most dangerous. They go too far without meaning to."

Bonnie stood, turned so she was facing him.

"The wisdom of Rudy Manuel," she said.

Their kiss was long and fiery—the kiss of new lovers who'd been kept at arm's length for days on end. Bonnie was only mildly disturbed by the fact that she felt no guilt.

Rudy pulled back, smiled.

"I swear," he said, "I never did this with the Edwards Group."

CHAPTER 7

THE NEXT MORNING WAS sunny and mild. Bonnie decided to spend the day adding markers to the section of a hiking trail where several of her guests had lost their way. The trail led from the backside of the meadow upslope through forest dense with sequoias to a waterfall fed by a winding creek. The cascade itself was so small that no one had bothered to name it, but Bonnie found the algae coloring the surrounding stone mesmerizing, and the sound of the water itself was calming even on the most stressful of days. She loaded the markers, nails, and a hammer into one compartment of her Swiss Army backpack, and a picnic lunch complete with an airline-sized bottle of red wine into the other.

She set out at a little after eight a.m., knowing full well that there were more important things she could be doing. The guests who'd complained were intoxicated at the time, and she was pretty sure the incident wouldn't repeat itself. But this was the best excuse she had to give herself the kind of day she needed after an awful, high-anxiety forty-eight hours. She needed to reconnect with the mountains, to remind herself of why she'd fallen in love with Camp Nelson in the first place.

Most important, she needed to be alone. Away from Jim and Rudy and even the kids. Away from demanding guests. Away from phones and fax machines. Someplace where she couldn't be reached and wouldn't be disturbed. It wasn't that she wanted to think—she wanted to take a break from thinking.

According to her inebriated guests, the trickiest part of the trail came in the long stretch between two granite outcroppings. The forest was thick and steep there, and the path was continually covered with a fresh layer of duff. Bonnie passed the first outcropping and had to admit that it was harder to pick the trail back up than she'd remembered. The markers were scarce, and as she hiked upslope she sometimes had the sensation that she'd gone off course and was simply standing in the middle of an untamed forest. More than once she had to backtrack, return to the first set of rocks, and start over.

In theory, it was impossible to get lost since at least one of the two outcroppings was never more than a few steps from view, but Bonnie could understand how, if you ventured here in the dark, or in an altered state, you might start to panic. And her guests had spoken the truth: there were no markers to be found anywhere. It was, Bonnie thought, simply a matter of spelling out the straightest line possible between the two clusters of granite. From there, the trail became crystal clear as it followed the creek the last mile up to the waterfall.

She chose a place to start, knelt down, and opened her backpack. The markers she'd brought with her were oval reflectors like the ones you'd find on the back of a bicycle. Shine your flashlight around until some of that light came back at you, and you shouldn't have any difficulty at all.

Her plan for the day was succeeding. She lost herself in the sun and shade, the quiet, the thin mountain air. Sometimes she would remember where she was and think: *I'm kneeling at the base of a 140-foot tree, five thousand miles above sea level. This is my life now. This is the life I've made.* When she was done working, she would continue on to the waterfall. She knew exactly where she'd spread her blanket and eat. She could already feel the wine moving through her body, warming her from the inside. And then she would lay back, shut her eyes, and listen to the water.

She was about halfway done when she heard a birdcall she didn't recognize coming from maybe a hundred yards below. It sounded to her like the highest pitch of a tin whistle played in a long-short-short pattern. She was tempted hike back down and see if she could identify the species, but then she heard the same call coming from roughly the same distance in the opposite direction.

They must be talking about me, she thought. *Warning the forest that there's an intruder.*

She smiled, took a sip of water, went back to work.

But then what had to be another of the same kind of bird perched somewhere to the east joined the conversation, repeating the exact same call. She stood and listened, trying to envision the bird: she guessed small, maybe the size of her fist, and yellow-breasted with black wings. She wanted very badly to see one, to know if what she pictured was accurate.

She tried to talk back to them by imitating their call, but her attempt came out breathy and uneven. Still, they responded, or seemed to, with each bird sounding off in rapid succession. Not only that, but she was sure they were inching closer. She tried her hand at their call again—tried, even though she knew it was impossible, to make her version sound friendly, nonthreatening.

But her whistling appeared to rattle the birds. Their song altered. The pitch dipped an octave lower; the long opening note dropped off. And then the call changed completely. Instead of a single pitch there were two, one high and one low, and the sound no longer resembled a tin whistle. More like a parrot imitating human speech, Bonnie thought.

And then she understood: these weren't birds closing in on her.

She concentrated until the two short syllables came into focus: *rich bitch, rich bitch, rich bitch.* From the north, the south, the east. *Rich bitch, rich bitch, rich bitch.* One at a time, and then in unison.

They were on her now, no farther than twenty feet in each direction. She could see them darting between the trees, bandanas hiding their faces as if they were grown men playing cops and robbers.

Despite herself, Bonnie screamed. And then she grabbed her backpack and ran, the voices behind her chirping *rich bitch, rich bitch, rich bitch* all the way to the meadow.

CHAPTER 8

A WEEK HAD PASSED since the incident at Camp Nelson Saloon, and Bonnie was determined to put in another appearance. She walked the access road at a little after sundown. Rudy followed close behind.

"You don't need to prove anything to anyone," he said. "Least of all that inbred trash."

"That's where you're wrong," Bonnie said. "They can't think I'm backing down."

"Then let me go alone."

"Ha! Thanks, but I don't feel like making a trip to the hospital or the morgue tonight. Besides, they need to see my face. If I send you, it looks worse than if I do nothing at all."

"And what if they decide to start something? How are you going to—"

"I'll play it by ear."

They walked the rest of the way without talking. At first glance, it seemed Bonnie had already won. Apart from

Kelly and a large red-haired biker at the far end of the bar, the place was empty.

"Looks like they're trying to hit me in my wallet," Bonnie said.

"Or maybe it's just early," Rudy said.

"Let's find out."

They sat dead-center at the bar, took two of the same stools the delinquent bikers had occupied a week earlier.

"Evening ma'am," Kelly said. "Rudy. What can I get you all tonight?"

Bonnie remembered how Kelly had smirked while she wiped beer from her pants. She decided to have a little fun at her employee's expense.

"I could really go for an Old Fashioned," she said.

"That a microbrew?" Kelly asked.

"It's a cocktail. Part bitters, part... You know, never mind. I'll just take a Manhattan."

Kelly gave a blank stare. Rudy covered his grin.

"How about a Sidecar?" Bonnie asked.

"This is a beer and shots bar, ma'am," Kelly said.

"Well, I guess we'll need to fix that, won't we?" Bonnie said, smiling. "Meanwhile, pour me a Pilsner."

"I'll take a Jameson, on the rocks," Rudy said.

They carried their drinks to a nearby table. Bonnie sat down, then popped back up.

"There's something sticky on my seat," she said, reaching for a napkin. "I'm telling you, that woman really needs to go. And this jukebox needs an overhaul. Or at least a song with more than three chords."

"Country and Western sells booze," Rudy said. "More than rock or pop or jazz. That's a fact. There have been studies."

"Well, maybe we don't need a bar at all," Bonnie said.

"Let's take one thing at a time."

They were quiet for a while, Bonnie casting glances at the door, Rudy staring down into his drink, giving the ice an occasional stir.

"No family this weekend?" he asked.

Bonnie frowned. "Jim says he won't bring the kids back until it's safe. Can you believe that? He's never thought twice about anyone's safety—he just wants to drive a wedge between me and this place."

Rudy went back to poking at the ice in his glass, pushing a cube down with his straw and then watching it float back up.

"You know you're supposed to drink that, not play with it," Bonnie said.

Rudy's smile looked more like a grimace.

"I'm out of practice," he said. "To be honest, I kind of gave it up when I moved out here. I guess you could say that I moved out here in order to give it up."

"I'm sorry," Bonnie said. "I had no idea. I'll take these back and get us two Cokes."

"No, it's all right," Rudy said. "I'm ready now. I'm all grown up. I should be able to enjoy a drink like anybody else."

"You should be able to, or you are?"

"I am."

"You're sure?"

"I'm sure. I promise."

He lifted his glass in a toast.

"To growing up," he said.

They drank, then sat grinning sheepishly at one another.

"Let me ask you something," Bonnie said.

"Shoot."

"You've been living out here for a while now. Does it ever get old? Are you still happy?"

"Happier now than ever," Rudy said, winking.

"That's not what I mean," Bonnie said. "You could have met a girl anywhere. Do you miss...civilization? Do you ever feel like you made a big mistake?"

"If I felt that way, I'd leave," Rudy said. "But this is where I belong. I'm a better person now. I'm better because of this place."

"You mean because you stopped drinking?"

"That's part of it."

"What's the other part?"

Rudy tapped his glass.

"I'll need a few more before I answer that one."

"How about this? How about we have one more, then take a late-night stroll up to the lake?"

"That's why you're the boss," Rudy said. "You have all the good ideas."

Bonnie looked over her shoulder, signaled to Kelly for another round. The clock above the bar read ten p.m.

"Seems like they really are boycotting me," she said. "Honestly, it's a relief. I'm going to remake the place from top to bottom. A high-end bar for discerning guests. A bartender who knows how to make a Manhattan."

She wondered if the bikers realized they'd gone too far that morning in the woods. Maybe they'd scared themselves off. Maybe they expected the cops to come swooping down if they set foot anywhere near Camp Nelson Lodge.

"Hold that thought," Rudy said, cupping a hand to his ear.

Bonnie listened, caught the roar of approaching motorcycles. Sure enough, the bikers came filing in a short time later, the same gaggle Rudy had tossed out the week before. It looked to Bonnie like they'd been drinking already. The towering rabble-rouser in the red bandana wobbled as he walked, and his entourage was cackling like a gang of teenage girls.

"Hey, Kelly," the leader called, "line 'em up. And crank up the music while you're at it."

Rudy leaned across the table.

"What do you want to do?" he whispered.

Bonnie shrugged.

"It's a new day in a free country, right?" she said. "We sit here and enjoy our drinks."

She got ready to be stared down, called names, laughed at, even spit on. But they walked past her table without so much as acknowledging her or Rudy. Bonnie watched them gather their drinks at the bar, then huddle around a nearby table.

"You want to take that walk now?" Rudy asked.

"Uh-uh, no way," Bonnie said. "We stay right here until they leave."

"All right, as long as you don't mind being seen out and about with the help. Especially the male help."

"I don't mind at all," Bonnie said. "Anyway, it looks like they've come to their senses."

"It's a little early to make that call," Rudy said.

Two hours and four rounds later, the bikers were the last of the paying customers to leave. They mouthed an ominous "Goodnight" to Bonnie and Rudy on their way out but were otherwise well behaved.

"Maybe they really have come around," Rudy said.

Bonnie laughed.

"What's so funny?" Rudy asked.

"You're slurring your words."

"I told you, it's been a while."

"And it's been a long time since I took advantage of a drunk guy. Why don't I steer you back to my cabin?"

Rudy smiled.

"As long as you promise to take advantage of me," he said.

CHAPTER 9

"SOME PEOPLE GO TO church on Sunday mornings," Sergeant Wylie said.

"Yeah, and some people sleep past sunrise," his partner O'Dowd said.

They turned onto the access road and headed for Camp Nelson. It was a perfect California morning, clear and crisp with nothing moving or making a sound save the occasional bird dive-bombing an earthworm. O'Dowd slowed the car as they passed the saloon.

"Nothing doing there," Wylie said.

But then they emerged from the forest into the clearing and the quiet morning seemed like a distant memory. There were squad cars with their lights spinning parked at random intervals all around the property. Uniform officers moved in and out of the cabins, interviewing guests. Men and women in lab coats were unpacking the forensics van. It was hard to tell what the police tape was meant to keep in and what it was meant to keep out.

"Looks like we found the action," Wylie said.

"Yeah," O'Dowd said, "and it looks like they started without us."

He pulled up behind last squad car and cut the engine.

"You're the primary on this one, right?" he asked.

Wylie glared at him.

"You know, for someone so young you're awfully damn lazy," he said.

"I'm forty-four."

"You've got time yet. I didn't start phoning it in till I turned fifty."

A trooper fresh from the academy handed them two pairs of latex gloves and scrub booties.

"Main scene's over there," he said, pointing to Bonnie's cabin.

"You mean the bodies?" O'Dowd asked.

"Yes sir. Or at least one body. The other vic is still breathing."

"I thought we had two DOAs," Wylie said.

"Well, by the time you walk over there you might," the trooper said. "The woman's all the way dead, but the male is touch and go."

Wylie and O'Dowd looked at each other, then turned and ran. They shouldered their way through a circle of lab coats and burst into the cabin, both of them breathing hard. A pair of EMTs were preparing Rudy for transit. They'd wrapped a thick bandage around his skull and fitted his head into a foam contraption that looked to O'Dowd like the packaging his stereo had come in.

"Can he talk?" Wylie asked.

"He's been shot in the head," the lead EMT said. "You'll be lucky if he ever talks again."

Wylie leaned over the stretcher.

"You mean to tell me this son-of-a-bitch has a bullet in his brain and he's still alive?" he asked.

"I can't say for sure if it hit the brain or not."

"Any chance he'll recover?" O'Dowd asked.

"There's always a chance," the EMT said. "But I wouldn't count on it."

Wylie and O'Dowd watched them wheel Rudy away, then turned to the bed. Bonnie lay on her back with her legs tangled beneath her. The wall behind the bed was spattered with blood and brain matter.

"She had no chance at all," O'Dowd said.

"Yeah, it was over real quick for her."

A crime scene photographer neither of them had noticed before stepped to the foot of the bed and began snapping pictures.

"Hey, take a look at this," O'Dowd said, pointing to the nightstand. "We've got a stuffed money clip, a knockoff Rolex, and a silver cross."

"Huh," Wylie said. "Definitely not a robbery."

"Nope," O'Dowd said. "Not that anyone would have come all the way out here to rob just one cabin."

"So we're looking at an intentional hit."

"One of them was the target, anyway. Could be the other one was collateral damage."

"Doesn't make our job any easier."

O'Dowd shrugged.

"Let's hope our hitman forgot to wear gloves."

* * *

Without the kids in tow, Jim managed to make the four-hour drive in just under three hours. He sped into the clearing, parked his Mercedes among the squad cars, and ran for Bonnie's cabin.

"Where is she?" he yelled. "Is she in there? Is my wife in there?"

Someone reached out and caught his arm as he ducked under the police tape. It was Wylie.

"Sir," he said, "we're still investigating. This is as far as I can let you go."

"What are you talking about? I own this place. They told me my wife is dead."

"You're Mr. Hood?"

Jim nodded.

"God," he said. "I feel like I'm going to pass out."

"Why don't we have a seat over here in my car," Wylie said. "I'll have someone bring you a bottle of water."

He snapped his fingers at a passing uniform cop, then handed him a dollar.

"Let's get this man some water," he said. "There's a vending machine in the lodge."

"Yes sir."

Jim sat on the passenger's side, Wylie behind the wheel. Jim scanned the property. So much trouble, he thought, over a backwoods dump. Even if Bonnie had made improvements.

"What happened?" he asked.

"What did they tell you?"

"Only that Bonnie was dead. That she'd been killed."

Wylie cleared his throat. He wished like hell it had been O'Dowd standing there when the husband came charging up the path.

"She was shot," he said, "late last night or early this morning."

"Jesus Christ."

"There's more," Wylie continued. "There's no easy way to say this, so I'll just come out with it: your wife wasn't alone."

Jim cocked his head like he was struggling to comprehend what Wylie had just told him.

"What do you mean? Was someone else hurt?"

"Rudy Manuel, her handyman. It looks like they were in bed together when the shooter—"

"You're telling me Bonnie was with another man? I don't believe it. Not with him. Not with that little..."

Wylie studied him out of the corner of one eye. The tears were real. The confusion seemed real, too.

The officer returned with a bottle of water. Wylie passed it to Jim, waited while he took a long swig.

"I'm sorry," he said, "but I have to ask: you really didn't know your wife was having an affair?"

Jim struck the dashboard with the palm of one hand.

"Of course I didn't," he said.

"Easy now," Wylie said. "I'm not judging. Things happen in a marriage."

"Not in my marriage. We have two kids. We built a small empire together. Bonnie wasn't going to risk all that for a fling with a glorified vagrant."

He'd said more than he meant to. He looked over at Wylie, found no hint of suspicion or blame.

"It was those bikers," Jim said.

"Bikers?"

Jim told Wylie about the brick through the Jeep window, the threatening notes, the confrontation at the Camp Nelson Saloon. He spoke quickly, his voice breaking now and again, his forehead damp with sweat.

"I see," Wylie said.

"You see what? Why didn't you people protect her? Isn't that your job?"

I could ask the same of you, Wylie thought.

"Listen, Mr. Hood," he said, "why don't you go get a cup of coffee in the lodge? I'll come talk to you again in a little bit, when I know more. If you like, I could have an officer sit with you."

"I'd rather be alone," Jim said.

He didn't bother to shut the door behind him. Wylie watched him walk across the property, then went looking for O'Dowd. He found his partner on the phone in Bonnie's cabin. O'Dowd nodded, held up one hand.

"Got it," he said into the receiver. "Thank you, that could be a big help."

He hung up, looked over at Wylie.

"Did you get anything off the husband?" he asked.

"Not really," Wylie said. "Only that he was quick to point the finger. What was that call about? You sounded almost hopeful."

"I don't know if it's good news or bad," O'Dowd said. "Our living vic has quite a rap sheet. Including a five-year stint for armed robbery."

"Well now, that's interesting. Could be he crossed the wrong people and was hiding out up here."

"Could also be a red herring."

Wylie nodded.

"Let's hope Mr. Manuel's feeling chatty when he wakes up," he said.

"*If* he wakes up," O'Dowd said.

CHAPTER 10

RUDY LAY IN A hospital bed in a private room with a bandage wrapped tight around his skull and a brace holding his head and neck still. An IV ran from one arm. A computer monitor charted his vitals. His eyes were shut and had been for the more than two hours Wylie and O'Dowd sat with him. Wylie dozed in a plastic armchair, slipping in and out of a recurring nightmare that saw him go bankrupt just months into his retirement. O'Dowd kept one eye on their witness and the other on an episode of *Three's Company*. The room smelled like menthol and rubber, and O'Dowd wondered what exactly he was breathing in.

Rudy stirred a little, his nostrils flaring and his fingers twitching, and then came to.

"Hey," O'Dowd said, snapping fingers. "Hey, he's awake."

Wylie rubbed at his eyes, then pushed himself out of the chair.

"But is his brain working?" he asked.

"Only one way to find out."

They stood on opposite sides of the bed, watching. At first, Rudy seemed conscious but unaware, as if he didn't know where he was or what had happened to him and was too far gone to ask questions. Little by little, though, his eyes started to focus. He took in his surroundings as best he could without moving his head, then tried to speak but found his mouth too dry.

"The nurse said it would be okay to give him a sip of water," O'Dowd told Wylie.

He stuck a straw in a Styrofoam cup, transferred water from a green pitcher, and held the cup out to Rudy. The act of pursing his lips seemed to cause Rudy pain, but with a little effort he managed to drink.

"Thank you," he said, his voice strained, feeble.

O'Dowd wondered if the bruising and swelling around Rudy's eyes were caused by the surgery or the bullet itself.

"Do you know who I am?" O'Dowd asked.

Rudy raised one hand and pointed to the badge hanging from O'Dowd's jacket pocket.

"Cops," he said.

"Do you know where you are? And how you got here?" Wylie asked.

Rudy tried to nod, found himself restricted by the brace.

"Yes," he whispered.

Wylie and O'Dowd exchanged encouraging glances.

"Can you tell us who did this to you?" O'Dowd asked.

Rudy moved his jaw back and forth as though preparing to speak in full sentences.

"Bonnie?" he asked. "Is she..."

O'Dowd started to answer, but Wylie held up a hand: best not get him excited.

"We don't know yet," Wylie said. "What's important now is that we find who did this."

Rudy shut his eyes again, either with relief or with the strain of trying to remember.

"I don't know," he said.

"You didn't see him before he fired?" O'Dowd asked.

"It was dark. He was in the shadows."

"So there was just one assailant?" Wylie asked.

"Yes."

"Did you notice anything about him at all?"

"He was tall," Rudy said. "Maybe six four. And big. Very big."

"Fat big, or scary big?" O'Dowd asked.

"Scary big."

"Any big, shadowy men in your past?" Wylie asked.

"What do you mean?"

Words seemed to be coming a bit more easily. He seemed to want to cooperate.

"We've had a look at your rap sheet, Mr. Manuel," Wylie said. "You're more or less a career criminal."

"Uh-uh. I've been clean a long time now."

"So you switched careers. Still, sometimes a criminal's past will only stay buried for so long. Maybe someone you double-crossed just got out. Maybe someone you robbed had trouble tracking you down."

Rudy attempted to clench his fists but couldn't find the strength.

"No," he said. "There's no one."

"You're sure?" O'Dowd asked. "You can't think of a single soul who would want to hurt you?"

"Not like that."

"What do you mean?"

"Anyone who'd want to do me would come straight at me. They'd have something to say. They'd want something from me first. This guy just started firing."

"Your blood alcohol was sky high," Wylie said. "Could be you're blanking on the conversation."

"No. I remember."

"You remember anything else?" O'Dowd asked. "Anything at all."

Rudy took a minute to think.

"His hair was long and curly. I saw it in his shadow against the wall."

"Any chance you could give us a color?"

"No."

"All right, Mr. Manuel," Wylie said. "We'll let you get some rest. But chances are we'll be back with more questions."

Rudy shut his eyes, already drifting back into sleep.

* * *

The detectives sat on a bench in the hall outside Rudy's room and compared notes.

"I wish it didn't, but his story makes sense," Wylie said.

"How so?"

"If the shooter was one of his old running bunnies, the cash and jewelry wouldn't have been sitting there for us to find. A career thief doesn't take a pass just because robbery wasn't on the agenda that day."

"So you believe him when he says he didn't get a good look at the guy?" O'Dowd asked.

"I do."

"Where does that leave us?"

Wylie rubbed at his eyes like he was still half dozing.

"You know," he said, "some witnesses reported seeing a tall biker type at the saloon on Saturday night. They thought he had to be waiting for someone, but he just sat there by himself drinking bottles of Heineken all night. It isn't the kind of place people just stumble on."

"Maybe he was a guest," O'Dowd offered.

"Maybe, but his description doesn't fit the bill. Bonnie was turning the lodge into a yuppie getaway. The registry shows all families that weekend. There were more kids on the property than adults."

They were quiet for a minute, each trying to figure their next move.

"It's a long shot," O'Dowd said, "but let's have forensics go over Saturday night's beer bottles with a fine-tooth comb. Maybe our guy's in the system. If he is our guy."

"Can't hurt," Wylie said. "Meanwhile, let's make sure we know everything there is to know about Mr. Jim Hood."

CHAPTER 11

THE FUNERAL AND VIEWING were finally over. Everything about the day felt wrong to Jim, like it had been meant for someone other than Bonnie. She'd never been a churchgoer. The cross and the stained glass and the pews and the strange attire of the man addressing the crowd all seemed to confuse his children. Mindy in particular couldn't wrap her brain around the fact that her mother was lying a few feet away in that closed box. Jim Jr. let out a tremendous sneeze every time the altar boy waved his incense.

It was Bonnie's parents who'd demanded a traditional service. They had never approved of Jim beyond his finances, especially not his mother-in-law, whose previously snide comments turned downright hostile after her daughter's death. "You should have been there with her, you know," she'd said at church that morning. "But then I suppose Bonnie went up there to get away from you." She wasn't being malicious: she was simply too devastated to worry about Jim's feelings.

Family, friends, colleagues, and neighbors were gathered now at the Hood home. The children appeared more at ease with so many familiar faces joined in a familiar setting. Jim Jr. sat on his grandfather's lap and played with a Rubik's Cube. Mindy, without asking permission, changed out of her dress and into her favored jeans and a T-shirt. Jim had the event catered, but Bonnie's mother insisted on making ambrosia, which she claimed was Bonnie's favorite childhood dessert though Jim had never seen his wife eat so much as a spoonful.

He'd hoped to open the backyard to guests, but it was a rare overcast night in SoCal. Even the Hoods' sprawling and well-furnished living room couldn't quite accommodate upwards of fifty people. Guests spilled into the family room, the kitchen, even the master bedroom. Jim mingled, listening to condolences and fond memories, nodding and smiling where appropriate, saying little, keeping each conversation brief. The facts of Bonnie's death—in particular the fact of Rudy—had made the papers. Jim felt people looking at him with two expressions at once, as though attempting to mirror the mix of shame and grief they believed he must be feeling.

As the night wore on and people continued drinking, Jim seemed to become more and more invisible. He overheard things, the kind of things no one would have said to his face, though he wondered if deep down they wanted him to hear.

"You can't blame her," a friend of Bonnie's told someone Jim didn't recognize. "She was faithful to him for all those years, and he barely paid any attention to her outside of the business."

"Maybe it wasn't Jim who pulled the trigger, but it might as well have been," said a cousin Jim had seen maybe a half-dozen times in his life.

Bonnie's mother, after a few glasses of sherry, went even further: "Someone paid to have my daughter killed, and I know damn well who that someone is."

It was the same wherever Jim went in the house. He needed to calm down. He needed a stiff drink. He was standing in the kitchen, filling his glass with ice, when the worst possible thought occurred to him: What if the children were overhearing these conversations, too? He tossed his glass in the sink, looked around frantically, then ran down the hall and burst into living room. He found Mindy and Jim Jr. sitting on floor with Bonnie's brother, playing a game of Chinese Checkers, Jim Jr.'s latest obsession.

"Kids, kids," Jim called, louder than he meant to. "It's getting late. I think we need to start saying goodbye to our guests."

"Just let us finish this game," Jim Jr. said.

Jim felt panicked, like the boy's failure to act quickly might somehow cost another life.

"Now," he said.

Despite himself, he could feel his face turning red and his jaws flexing.

"Your mother's dead, and you're sitting there playing a game," he shouted. "What the hell's wrong with you?"

He scanned the faces in the room, saw the makings of an angry mob staring back at him.

CHAPTER 12

THE TULARE COUNTY HOMICIDE Bureau, with its fake wood paneling and softball league pennants, looked like a semifinished basement though it sat on the second floor of Camp Nelson's municipal building. O'Dowd had to turn sideways in order to shuffle through a hallway jammed with mismatched filing cabinets. He entered a room full of cluttered desks and disgruntled detectives and shouted Wylie's name from the opposite side of the floor.

"I'm trying to work here," Sergeant Sandercoe protested from across the room.

"Oh please," O'Dowd said. "Like you know how to do anything on that computer besides play solitaire."

O'Dowd reached Wylie's desk and took a moment to catch his breath.

"You all right there?" Wylie asked.

"You aren't going to believe this," O'Dowd said. "We got a hit. Off those bottles."

"The Heineken bottles?"

"Yeah. A guy named Bruce Beauchamp from Fontana. Construction worker by day, drug dealer by night. He has a page and a half worth of priors. And get this: he's six four, 240 pounds, and has curly hair."

"Not bad," Wylie said. "Any connection to Rudy Manuel?"

"Too early to say, but I doubt it. They did their stints at different facilities, and they went away for different crimes."

"We have an address for Mr. Beauchamp?"

"A trailer park halfway down the coast to LA."

"All right, then," Wylie said. "Let's get the cavalry lined up."

* * *

They met the local task force at five the next morning, in the parking lot of an abandoned strip mall three miles from Beauchamp's trailer camp. The sheriff's office sent three squad cars and a SWAT van.

"Seems like a lot for just one guy," O'Dowd told Sergeant Sandercoe, the SWAT team leader.

"These trailer parks can turn into combat zones real quick," Sandercoe said. "Our incident commander doesn't like us taking chances."

Wylie guzzled his coffee.

"Fine by me," he said. "I gave up on guts and glory a long time ago."

The sergeant spread out a map of the trailer park on the hood of O'Dowd's sedan and drew a circle around Beauchamp's home with a red marker.

"We'll serve the warrant," he said. "You hang back here, at the park's entrance. Once we've got him in cuffs, he's all yours."

O'Dowd yawned.

"He boring you?" Wylie asked.

"I'm a night owl by nature," O'Dowd said. "Coffee doesn't work for me before the sun's up."

O'Dowd and Wylie made the short drive sandwiched between SWAT's unmarked van and the three squad cars. They peeled off at the entrance, cut the sedan's headlights, and sat waiting for the go-ahead to come over the radio.

They didn't have to wait long. By the time Wylie tore the cellophane off a fresh pack of cigarettes and lit one, the sergeant's voice was already summoning them through a haze of static.

"Beauchamp must not be a fighter," O'Dowd said.

"Let's hope he coughs up his confession that quick."

They found him sitting on the makeshift stoop in front of his broken-down trailer, hands cuffed behind his back. He wore a stained tank top and an old pair of jeans, and his curly red hair was clearly fresh off the pillow. Sergeant Sandercoe stood over him like he was the prize at the end of a big-game hunt.

"He give you any trouble?" O'Dowd asked.

"No sir," Sandercoe said. "Had a Glock on the nightstand, but he slept right through us kicking the door in."

"I thought felons weren't allowed to have guns," Wylie said, for Beauchamp's benefit.

"You know, I don't believe they are," O'Dowd said. "I believe that's what you call a violation."

"I got no clue what you guys are doing here," Beauchamp said, without much conviction.

"We'll tell you all about it in the car," Wylie said. "Right after we read you your rights."

"I know my rights."

"I guess you would by now," O'Dowd said. "Come on, let's go."

Beauchamp stood, seeming to keep rising well past the six foot four Rudy had described. Wylie had to slide the passenger seat forward in order to fit him in the back of the sedan. Neighbors stepped outside to watch, the men bare-chested and the women in curlers. Their expressions were none too friendly.

"Sandercoe wasn't kidding," O'Dowd said under his breath.

"Yeah, let's scat," Wylie said.

The sun was starting to show by the time they hit the highway. Wylie and O'Dowd had planned to say as little as possible until they got back to the station, but Beauchamp wouldn't have it.

"I'm hungry and I gotta piss," he complained. "This is cruel and unusual."

"Pipe down," Wylie said.

"Where are you taking me? At least tell me that much."

"Someplace you've been before."

"I've been a lot of places. And I didn't break any laws. What you're doing right now is called kidnapping. State-sanctioned kidnapping."

"We're going to have a nice, civilized conversation," O'Dowd said. "That's all."

"Then let's have it here. Go ahead and ask your questions. I got nothing to hide."

"All right," Wylie said, pivoting in his seat. "Why don't you tell us what you were doing up at Camp Nelson two Saturdays ago?"

"That what this is about? A working man can't take a weekend to himself without getting dragged to the precinct house?"

"No offense, Mr. Beauchamp, but you don't strike me as the kind of guy who has the luxury of weekend R&R," Wylie said.

"Why? 'Cause I live in a trailer? I make more in a month than you two put together."

"Like I said, Mr. Beauchamp…"

"So I guess you're Tulare County cops? That where we're headed? Camp Nelson?"

"See, now you've ruined the surprise," Wylie said.

Beauchamp perked up a little, like he saw an advantage in dealing with backwoods cops.

"What is you think I did up there?"

"I got a better idea," O'Dowd said. "Why don't you tell us what you did up there?"

"All right. A friend from the job site told me about the place. I'd been having trouble with my girl and needed to clear my head. A weekend of fishing and hiking seemed like just the thing."

"No drinking?"

"Yeah, some of that, too."

"Where?"

"I don't know if the place even had a name. It was down a country road, way off the beaten path."

"How'd you find it?"

"Desk clerk where I was staying suggested I check it out. He drew me a map."

"Where were you staying?"

"Motel Six. Go ahead and check their records."

"We will," Wylie said. "Meanwhile, what's your friend's name? The one who recommended Camp Nelson."

"John."

"What's John's last name?"

"I don't know."

"You don't know?"

"We're work friends. We talk on our lunch break, that's all."

"So if we show up at the site on Monday morning we'll be able to find this John?" O'Dowd asked.

"Maybe."

"Maybe?"

"He's a day worker. He goes wherever they send him."

"But your foreman would know how to reach him, right?" O'Dowd followed up.

"I guess."

"What about your girl?" Wylie asked. "She have a name? A number?"

Beauchamp sunk down, pushed his knees against the back of Wylie's seat. They'd made it clear that he was in for the long haul.

"You know what?" he said. "Why don't you guys call and get me a lawyer. I'm gonna rest up now. Make sure I got my wits about me."

"That's a good idea, Mr. Beauchamp," Wylie said. "The best one I've heard in a while."

CHAPTER 13

JIM JR. AND MINDY sat finishing their breakfast at the kitchen table while their father talked on the phone with a Camp Nelson detective. They watched him pace the floor, wandering as far away as the phone cord would allow, then retracing his steps. Now and again he would ask a question—*So he's not local? How long has he been out? But he hasn't confessed?*—then nod intently while he listened to the answers.

"Sounds like they caught the guy who shot Mommy," Jim Jr. said.

"Shush," Mindy told him.

She walked over to her father and whispered, "Daddy, what is it?"

"Can you hold on a second?" Jim said into the receiver.

"Why don't you kids wait for me in the living room?" he said. "The cartoons should be on now."

"But Daddy—"

"I'll be right there."

Mindy stayed put. Jim Jr. pretended not to hear.

"Now!" Jim said.

The children walked away at a snail's pace. Jim returned to his call.

"Just so I'm clear," he said, "you *have* made a formal arrest?"

"Yes sir, we have," Wylie confirmed.

"So you're confident it was this Beauchamp who killed Bonnie?"

"He wouldn't be in jail otherwise. Still, I'm not the judge or jury."

"And all you've got is a fingerprint?"

"We also have an eyewitness, Mr. Hood. One who seems to be getting stronger and remembering more every day."

"You mean the man who was sleeping with my wife?"

Wylie let the question pass.

"I'll be in touch when we know more," he said. "Meanwhile, feel free to call me any time."

Jim found Mindy and Jim Jr. sitting at attention on the couch, both of them too eager to speak or move. He crouched on the floor in front of them, put one hand on Mindy's arm and the other on Jim Jr.'s knee.

"I've got big news," he said. "They've arrested the man who killed your mother," he said.

"Told you!" Jim Jr. said.

Mindy ignored her brother.

"Who?" she asked. "Who is he?"

"Yeah, who is he?" Jim Jr. echoed.

Jim hesitated, not sure how much he should share or withhold.

"A man named Bruce Beauchamp," he said.

"Yeah, but who *is* he?" Mindy insisted.

"I don't really know," Jim said. "At least I don't know much. He's a construction worker. He's been in prison before."

"Are you going to kill him?" Jim Jr. asked, his voice full of hope.

"Ask a real question," Mindy said.

"That is a real question."

"No it isn't. The man's in jail already. You know Daddy can't kill him in jail."

"He could if—"

"Kids, kids," Jim interrupted. "No arguing, please."

They were quiet for a moment, as though arguing were their only means of communication, and then, to Jim's surprise, they began asking many of the same questions he'd asked Wylie.

"Why?" Jim Jr. wanted to know. "Why did he do it?"

"Did he know Mommy?" Mindy asked.

"Was he mad at her?"

Jim shook his head.

"I wish I had answers for you," he said. "I never heard of this man before."

"But he must have had a reason," Jim Jr. insisted.

"Bad guys have all kinds of reasons," Jim said. "They aren't always personal. Maybe he wanted to rob Mommy, and she wouldn't let him."

The explanation sounded lame to him, but he had nothing better to offer.

"How do the police know it was him?" Jim Jr. asked.

"Because of his fingerprints," Jim said. "They found them nearby."

"But did he say he did it?" Mindy asked.

"No. At least not yet."

"So there's just fingerprints?" Mindy pressed. "What if they have to let him go?"

Her eyes were welling up, and her voice sounded panicked. Jim Jr. seemed to catch her fear.

"No, no, no, sweetie," Jim said. "Fingerprints are—"

"What if they let him go and he gets in his car and comes looking for us?" Mindy asked.

"He wouldn't do that."

"Why not? If he wanted to kill Mommy, he must want to kill us, too."

Jim sucked in a long breath. He couldn't remember ever feeling so powerless to calm his own children.

"That's not how it works," he said. "Besides, the police won't let him go. They have more than fingerprints. They have an eyewitness. Someone who saw the man do it."

"Why didn't the witness stop him?" Jim Jr. asked.

"He tried," Jim said. "I have to give him that much. He tried."

CHAPTER 14

Six Months Later

RUDY TOOK THE STAND wearing a V-neck sweater and a collared shirt. The tip of a long and jagged surgical scar crept out from beneath his hairline, but otherwise he appeared fully recovered. Beauchamp sat beside his lawyer at the defendant's table, doodling in a legal pad. Jim couldn't say what made him more uncomfortable: having to keep his gaze on Rudy, the man who'd slept with his wife, for however long this cross examination would take; sitting just a few yards away from Beauchamp, the man who'd murdered his wife; or spending day after day sandwiched between his in-laws, who barely spoke to him.

The prosecutor had finished tossing softball questions at Rudy, and now it was the defense's turn. John Cotzee, Beauchamp's public defender, stood and scanned the jury, then stepped forward. He and his client were a study in contrasts. Beauchamp looked like Paul Bunyan stuffed into a double-breasted suit, while Cotzee was maybe five nine and weighed no more than 150 pounds. Beauchamp, in his late forties, still had a full head of wiry red hair; Cotzee, barely thirty, shaved his head to the bone. Beauchamp struggled to make eye contact and always appeared on the verge of blushing; Cotzee looked like the kid who was picked last for every team sport, but he had a sharp tongue and had already made several of the state's expert witnesses seem like stammering amateurs. Rudy was visibly rattled.

"Mr. Manuel," Cotzee started, "let's cut straight to the chase: you'd been drinking on the night you were shot and Mrs. Hood was killed, isn't that right?"

"I'd had a nightcap," Rudy said.

Cotzee gave a theatrical double-take.

"A nightcap?" he repeated. "I've read your medical records, Mr. Manuel. You had several DUIs worth of alcohol in your blood when the paramedics found you."

"Maybe it was more than one."

"You see, that worries me, Mr. Manuel. If you can't remember that much, how can we expect you to remember anything at all?"

"I remember just fine," Rudy said.

"We'll see. Why don't you start by walking us through that evening. What had you been drinking? And where? And with whom?"

Rudy cleared his throat, wiped a line of sweat from his upper lip.

"Whiskey," he said. "I'd been drinking whiskey at the Camp Nelson Saloon."

"With?"

"Bonn . . . Mrs. Hood."

Cotzee turned and pointed at Jim.

"In other words," he said, "you were on a date with this man's wife."

Jim did his best not to react.

"No," Rudy said. "It wasn't like that."

Cotzee raised one eyebrow.

"What was it like then?" he asked.

"I worked for Mrs. Hood. I was the property's caretaker. We'd been having trouble at the bar."

"Trouble?"

Rudy described the small gang of unruly bikers, focusing in particular on the beer their leader had dropped at Bonnie's feet.

"Was that the only incident with these bikers?" Cotzee asked.

"No," Rudy said. "There were others."

"In fact, Mrs. Hood had been receiving death threats for some time, all delivered on identical sheets of pale-blue paper. Isn't that right?"

Rudy nodded.

"One of these threats was wrapped around a brick and thrown through the windshield of her Jeep, isn't that also correct?"

"It is."

"And up until her death, you'd assumed it was this band of disgruntled bikers who'd been sending the threats?"

"Yes."

"A reasonable assumption. Mrs. Hood, in their view, was an outsider who sought to disrupt, if not outright destroy, their social hub. Camp Nelson Saloon had been their watering hole for a long, long time. Mrs. Hood wanted them gone. She wanted to replace them with Silicon Valley types. People with better manners and deeper pockets. Am I wrong?"

Rudy hesitated. There was more to the story, and the yes-or-no question left him flustered.

"She wanted to make the saloon part of the lodge," he said. "She wanted it to be for the guests."

"So she did want the locals gone?" Cotzee asked.

"Maybe, but—"

"Let's revisit your relationship with Mrs. Hood," Cotzee interrupted. "She was more than your employer, wasn't she?"

Rudy looked around the courtroom as though he'd written the answer somewhere on the walls.

"It's not a trick question, Mr. Manuel."

"We were friendly," Rudy said. "We liked each other."

"A little more than friendly," Cotzee sniggered. "You were sleeping with her, weren't you? In fact, the two of you had sex less than an hour before she was killed."

Murmurs broke out all around the courtroom. Rudy turned crimson.

"No," he said. "That's not right."

"So the police reports are wrong? You weren't found lying in your underpants on Mrs. Hood's bedroom floor?"

"Yes, but..." He sputtered out. Beauchamp lifted his head from the legal pad, looked surprised for the first time since the trial began. Jim didn't know who to root for.

"But what, Mr. Manuel?" Cotzee pressed.

Rudy looked down at his hands.

"I heard a noise. I came running."

"From where?"

"I was staying in the cabin next door. In case something happened."

Cotzee's eyebrows shot halfway up his forehead. There was more rumbling across the room. The judge issued a stern warning.

"So you *weren't* having an affair with Mrs. Hood?" Cotzee continued. "Is that what you're saying?"

Rudy squared his shoulders, leaned closer to the small microphone.

"We were friends. We both cared about the property. That's all."

"But that isn't what you told police," Cotzee said.

"I'd just been shot. Everything was fuzzy. I was confused."

"About whether or not you were sleeping with your very attractive and very wealthy boss?"

"I don't know. Maybe I wanted it to be true. Maybe my mind was playing tricks."

"Because you'd been shot in the head?"

"Yes. But now—"

"Let's recap, Mr. Manuel," Cotzee said. "You came here today to testify against Mr. Beauchamp, correct?"

"Yes."

"And how do you think your testimony is going so far?"

The prosecutor objected. The judge sustained.

"Withdrawn," Cotzee said. "But the fact remains, Mr. Manuel, that you've reversed your story on more than one key point, and there's more than ample reason to doubt your memory. First, you told the police it was dark that night and you couldn't see more than the assailant's silhouette. Earlier today, you told this court that you have no doubt it was Mr. Beauchamp standing in that room with the gun in his hand. Which is it?"

"It was him," Rudy said. "I'm sure it was him."

"Because you're one of those rare people whose memory improves with time and trauma?"

"I'm healed now. It all came back to me."

"I see. Still, it was dark that night, you were drunk, and then you were shot in the head. Isn't it at least possible that your memory of the shooting remains faulty?"

"I know what happened," Rudy said.

"Maybe. Do me a favor, would you? Give us a physical description of Mr. Beauchamp."

Rudy looked confused.

"That's him sitting right there," he said, pointing.

"Yes I know, but pretend he isn't there. Pretend I'm a sketch artist. What words would you use to describe Mr. Beauchamp?"

"Well, he's tall."

"Taller than six feet?"

"Yes."

"What else? What about his physique?"

"I'd say he's stocky. Big boned."

"Excellent. And how old would you say he is?"

"Between forty-five and fifty."

"Now, Mr. Manuel, how would you describe the customer who dropped his beer at Mrs. Hood's feet? A suspect you yourself introduced to this court."

Cotzee had done his homework. Rudy felt himself shrinking on the stand.

"I didn't say he was—"

"Please just answer the question. Was this man also taller than six feet?"

"Yes."

"Was he also big boned and stocky?"

"Yes."

"And would you say that he was also somewhere between forty-five and fifty?"

"Could be."

"Late at night, in the pitch dark and under the influence of a great deal of alcohol, mightn't it be difficult to tell them apart?"

"I guess, but—"

"At least as difficult as determining whether or not you'd been sleeping with the woman he murdered?"

"You're twisting my words. I—"

"Just be glad that I'm not allowed to discuss your own extensive arrest record, Mr. Manuel."

This time the prosecutor jumped to his feet.

"Withdrawn," Cotzee said. "I have nothing further for this witness."

Jim looked over at Beauchamp, caught the faintest hint of a grin.

CHAPTER **15**

"WHAT EXACTLY LED YOU to my client, Detective O'Dowd?" Cotzee asked.

O'Dowd, who'd stayed up all night rehearsing his testimony, then compensated for the lack of sleep by drinking a pot of coffee and three shots of espresso, explained in a jittery voice how witnesses from the saloon had led them to Beauchamp's fingerprint.

"And what was it witnesses noticed about my client?" Cotzee followed up.

"They thought his behavior was unusual."

"Unusual how?"

"He sat at the end of the bar, drinking alone. At first people thought he must be waiting for someone, but nobody came, and he didn't budge from his stool the whole night."

"Anything else?" Cotzee asked.

O'Dowd understood from Cotzee's tone how thin their path to Beauchamp must seem.

"Just that it isn't the kind of place people wander into," he said quickly. "It's off a small country road. Only locals know about it."

"And my client told you that a local recommended the place to him. Isn't that right?"

"Yes, but—"

"Have you ever had drink alone in a bar, Detective O'Dowd?"

"I guess so."

"And you weren't breaking the law, were you?"

"Of course not. That's not what—"

"Did any of your witnesses place Mr. Beauchamp at Mrs. Hood's cabin later that night?"

"No, they didn't."

"How about in the vicinity of the cabin?"

"No."

"Anywhere on the property other than saloon?"

"No."

"Were you able to establish any connection whatsoever between Mr. Beauchamp and Mrs. Hood?"

"Only that they spent most of that night in the same place."

"As did any number of people. Tell me, what was my client's motive for killing Mrs. Hood and shooting her lover? In your opinion."

"We think Mr. Beauchamp went to the saloon looking for a mark—someone to rob. He followed Mrs. Hood back to her cabin. He didn't expect to find Mr. Manuel there. Things went bad, and he panicked."

"You think? That all sounds awfully murky to me. I hate to use the term 'witch hunt,' but it fits here. Wouldn't you agree?"

"No," O'Dowd said. "I wouldn't."

"Really? You couldn't find a viable suspect, so you went after the one person the locals called strange, though really there was nothing at all strange about his behavior. It happens all the time: *He doesn't fit in, so he must have done it.* That kind of logic has landed more than one innocent man in prison, and of course it's the taxpayers who foot the bill."

"Mr. Beauchamp had a history of—"

"Of robbery, Detective O'Dowd. Mrs. Hood and Mr. Manuel weren't robbed, though their valuables, including a sizeable wad of cash, were lying in plain sight. So I'll ask again: do you have any physical evidence whatsoever linking my client to Mrs. Hood's murder? I mean apart from a fingerprint found a half-mile away from the crime scene."

O'Dowd hoped he didn't look as beaten as he felt. He hadn't expected to be put through the wringer by a public defender.

"Please answer the question, Detective O'Dowd," Cotzee said.

O'Dowd cleared his throat.

"We also had an eyewitness," he said.

"Ah, yes," Cotzee said. "An eyewitness who saw a 'tall, shadowy figure.' An eyewitness who offered police no description of his assailant until *after* you'd made an arrest.

We're all very familiar with Mr. Manuel. Like I said, what we have here is more witch hunt than investigation."

Jim watched O'Dowd leave the stand and exit the courtroom. As he turned back toward the judge, he locked eyes with Beauchamp. Neither man blinked or looked away until the next witness was called.

* * *

A few days later, it was all over. The jury deliberated for just an hour. When it was time for the verdict to be announced, Jim sat in his habitual front-row seat, flanked by his in-laws. The jury foreman, a retired postal worker in her mid-sixties, held up a piece of paper and took as long as humanly possible to read the phrase: "We the jury find the defendant . . . " After an equally lengthy pause, she added the phrase: "Not guilty."

Bonnie's mother let out a long wail that seemed to silence all other grumblings in the courtroom. Jim put hand on her shoulder; she swiped it away and recoiled into her husband's arms.

Jim turned to watch Beauchamp's reaction. He had Cotzee in a bear hug and was crying and smiling at once. Beauchamp spotted Jim watching and turned to face him. His smile dropped away. He had the look of a school bully who's spotted his prey from across the cafeteria. Jim locked eyes with his wife's killer for a second time. To his surprise, he felt more anger than fear.

CHAPTER 16

JIM AND THE KIDS made their final trip to Camp Nelson on a chilly Thursday in late October. Jim thought the occasion would mean more to the children if they were allowed to take off from school, and of course the trails would be less crowded on a weekday. He booked a suite in a nearby luxury hotel. They skirted the lodge, headed straight into mountains, and parked at a small trailhead. Mindy was out of the car before he'd cut the ignition. He leaned over and shook his son gently awake.

"Come on, buddy," he said.

Mindy wandered over to the nearest sequoia and placed both hands on the trunk as though the tree needed her support. Jim fetched his wife's urn from the trunk.

"Can I carry it?" Mindy called. "I want to be the one to carry it."

She came running over. Jim smiled. Mindy was like her mother: eager to tackle the most difficult part of any new task.

"Button up your jacket first," he said.

"Okay."

"And be very careful."

"I will," she said. "I promise."

They made the short hike up to an alpine lake Bonnie had called one of her greatest loves. The air was thin at this altitude, and Jim made an effort not to appear winded. When they reached the water, Mindy handed over the urn without his having to ask.

"There's no place she'd rather be," he said. "Especially on such a beautiful day."

Mindy began crying, softly; Jim Jr. put a hand on her back, then started bawling himself. Jim took off his shoes, waded out into the lake, unscrewed the top of the urn, and let his wife's ashes fall. Then they walked back to the car without saying a word.

* * *

Mindy sat in the back, staring out the window at the gorge below. Jim Jr. lasted just a few miles before he fell asleep. Jim focused his attention on a radio show about home repairs.

"Where are we going now?" Mindy asked.

"The hotel," Jim said.

"Why can't we stay at Mommy's lodge?"

"Because it isn't Mommy's lodge anymore."

"But why can't we keep it?" she asked.

Jim switched off the radio, looked over his shoulder.

"We talked about this," he said.

"I know," Mindy said. "I know it was Mommy's job. I know we can't keep it as a business. But we could go there on weekends, like before. It could be our summer house."

"Do you remember what it looked like the first time we visited? How it was all rundown and broken?"

"Yes," Mindy said, though really she'd fallen for the place at first sight, like her mother.

"Well, that's what happens when there isn't somebody to take care of it all the time. A place that big needs attention every day. It needs somebody to clean the rooms and fix things when they break. Somebody to water the flowers in the summer and clear the snow in the winter."

Mindy flashed on an idea, an idea that had been building since her mother's death.

"I could do it," she said.

"Do what?" Jim asked.

"Run the lodge. Water the flowers and clear the snow and clean the rooms."

Jim hid his grin.

"What about school?" he asked.

"I don't mean now," she said. "When I'm eighteen. It could be my job."

"With a brain like yours, you'll be headed to college when you're eighteen. You can be anything you want. A doctor. A lawyer. A professor."

"But I hate school. And I want to run the lodge."

"Honey, even if I agreed to hand the place over to you

on your eighteenth birthday, who's going to look after it in the meantime? It will go right back to the way it was before Mommy fixed it up."

He was growing tense. He heard his voice begin to strain.

"So I'll fix it back up," Mindy said.

Jim knew he should stop. There was no point in reasoning with an eleven-year-old who would likely have a new obsession in a week's time, but he felt inexplicably determined to close the subject, to know that he wouldn't have to dodge her pleas tomorrow at breakfast, and then again the day after, and the day after that.

"With what money?" he asked. "Repairs on a place like that cost a fortune."

Mindy thought it over.

"I'd pay you back," she said. "Once the lodge was making money again. It wouldn't take long at all."

Jim's patience cracked.

"Why?" he said. "Why in the world would you want to spend your life in the place that killed your mother?"

Mindy glared out from the backseat.

"This place didn't kill Mommy," she said. "Bruce Beauchamp did."

Jim gathered himself.

"I know, honey," he said. "It's hard to explain. If she hadn't been up here, if she'd stayed at home, then I would have been able to protect her. He wouldn't have been able to—"

"But he did and you didn't," Mindy shouted. "And now

he's free and he's going to come after us, and you can't do anything about it."

Jim Jr. startled awake. He sat staring at his father. Jim switched off radio, slowed to just below the speed limit.

"Listen," he said, "Bruce Beauchamp is a coward. Only a coward would hurt a woman. He won't come anywhere near us. It's over, you understand?"

Mindy crossed her arms and threw herself back against her seat.

"I understand," her brother said.

"Good," Jim said.

He switched the radio back on. He hated to admit it, but Mindy had spooked him. He glanced in the rearview mirror as though Beauchamp might be tailing them, then patted his jacket to make sure the .9mm handgun he'd purchased after the trial was still tucked in its holster.

CHAPTER 17

WHEN THEY GOT HOME on Friday night, the phone was ringing.

"I'll get it," Mindy said, sprinting into the kitchen.

Jim dragged their bags through the living room, then plopped down on the couch and switched on the television. Jim Jr. sat in the armchair and took up a handheld baseball game. Jim started to drift off when he heard the phone ring again.

"Mindy," he yelled, "I thought you were going to get it?"

He muted the television, heard Mindy speaking in her grown-up telephone voice.

"Hello, Hood residence," she said.

"Hello," she said again. "Hello?"

She came running into the living room as though someone were chasing her.

"Who was it?" Jim asked.

"I don't know," she said. "They hung up. Both times."

"Huh," Jim said.

"Daddy, I'm scared," Mindy said, climbing into his lap.

"Why, honey? It was probably just a wrong number."

"What if it was him?"

"If he was going to kill us, he wouldn't call first," Jim Jr. said, looking up from his game. "Unless maybe he wanted to make sure we were home."

Mindy stifled a little scream. Jim started to reprimand his son but stopped when he heard the phone ringing again.

"Let me go this time," he said, lifting Mindy off his lap.

But when he got to the kitchen, instead of answering, he pulled the cord from the phone and took the receiver off the hook. Then he lowered the volume on the answering machine, hit Play, and listened to a long string of hang ups.

Maybe Jim Jr. was right, he thought. *Maybe Beauchamp wants to make sure I'm home.*

He toured the house, checking that the windows and doors were all double locked.

Back in living room, he found his children sitting exactly as he'd left them, looking anxious and expectant.

"Let's have some fun this weekend," he said. "They're going to hold a fair at the beach tomorrow. Ferris wheels and game booths and cotton candy. How'd you like that?"

* * *

The boardwalk was crowded with people queuing up at the game booths and food booths and fortune-telling booths. Beyond the boardwalk, families spread out on the sand, the children building castles and forts, the adults scouting for shells.

Jim Jr. tugged on his father's sleeve and pointed to a shooting gallery.

"Can I, Dad? Please? I promise I'll give Mindy my prize."

"I can win my own prize," Mindy said.

"Sure," Jim said. "We're here to have fun, aren't we?"

"Me too?" Mindy asked. "I want to play, too."

"Both of you," Jim said. "When you're done, we'll find something to eat."

The game involved shooting duck cutouts with an air gun. Jim always marveled at how his son, whose grades demonstrated no great ability to focus, could lose himself instantly in the most trivial competition. Mindy eyed her brother, let him go first, tried to best him with every shot. Jim watched them, thinking this was the first real family day they'd had since Bonnie died. It was the first day they had nothing to do but be a family. No errands to run. No people to visit or entertain. Life would be good again, he thought. It would just take time.

In the end, Jim Jr. won a rubber whale and Mindy a stuffed porcupine.

They continued farther down the boardwalk and found a booth that sold pizza cones and funnel cakes. Jim bought three of each. They were eating and leaning against a railing when he spotted Beauchamp, or someone who could easily pass for Beauchamp, watching them from a distance. Jim nearly choked on his food. He stood up straight to get a better view, felt his gun pressing against his side.

He managed to stay calm while they finished their meal, talking in a cheery voice about nothing in particular and stealing the occasional glance, trying to determine if the person in question really was Beauchamp. The man was the right size and shape, and he seemed to return Jim's interest, but he was too far off to be sure; he might just be a stranger who wondered why Jim kept looking his way.

"Let's keep walking to the end," he told Mindy and Jim Jr. "You kids can run ahead if you want. Just don't run so far that you can't see me."

He watched them go, then pivoted with the intention of staring down Beauchamp, if it was Beauchamp. But the man was gone. He'd vanished, like the villain in a movie. Jim stood on his tiptoes and searched as far as he could see, but there was no trace. How could a man that tall and broad just disappear? At the very least, Jim should have been able to spot the hunting cap bobbing above the crowd. He wondered if his mind had been playing tricks, if all the sleepless nights since Bonnie died were catching up with him.

* * *

Back home, Jim checked the answering machine. This time there was a message. He looked around to make sure the children were out of earshot, then pressed Play. He recognized Beauchamp's voice immediately:

"I'll be at your office on Monday morning, and don't think you can brush me off 'cause I will sink you."

Jim listened to the message a second time before he erased it. His mind wasn't playing tricks: Beauchamp was coming for him.

CHAPTER 18

BRUCE BEAUCHAMP PARKED HIS rusty Nissan pickup among the BMWs and Mercedes-Benzes in the lot outside a four-story glass and steel building. This was a part of town he didn't know well, a part he associated with fat cats and corporate crime.

He set his sunglasses on the dashboard, looked at himself in the rearview mirror, then licked his palm and tamped down a cowlick sticking straight up from the center of his head.

He spotted four security cameras before he'd reached the automatic revolving door. The marble lobby featured a fountain and a half-dozen ficus trees.

A Muzak version of the Eagles' "Hotel California" played through hidden speakers.

Hood Realty was located on the third floor. Beauchamp pressed the elevator button, then decided to burn off some energy by taking the stairs.

At first glance, Jim Hood's office looked and smelled

like a doctor's waiting room. There were potted plants in every corner, silver-framed photos of luxury properties hanging on the walls, a mild odor of potpourri. It was the kind of place that tried hard not to offend and ultimately made no impression at all. The middle-aged receptionist in her beige pantsuit fit right in. She was working on a crossword puzzle and didn't seem to notice Beauchamp enter. He wished he'd worn something fancier—not a suit, necessarily, but maybe a V-neck sweater instead of his plaid button-down. Maybe she would have noticed him then. He walked over to her desk, cleared his throat.

"My name is Bruce Beauchamp," he said. "I have an appointment with Mr. Hood."

She smiled without looking up, pointed to a door on the opposite side of the waiting area.

"He's expecting you," she said.

"Thanks."

He felt off his game, out of his element. He turned his back to her, took a moment to gather himself, then marched into Jim's office and shut the door behind him. Jim was sitting at a large oak desk, studying some kind of spreadsheet. *A pencil pusher*, Beauchamp thought. *He doesn't stand a chance.* Jim moved back in his chair, gestured for Beauchamp to sit. Beauchamp shook him off.

"This won't take long," he said, leaning forward with both palms on desk. "I delivered on my end, but you—"

Jim held up a hand and smiled.

"I understand," he said. "I had some cash flow problems, but I'm delivering now."

He opened the center drawer of his desk, still smiling. Beauchamp stood up straight and seemed to relax. Without saying another word, Jim pulled out his .9mm handgun and fired twice into Beauchamp's forehead. Beauchamp fell straight back, landing with an impact that shook every object in the room. Jim walked around the desk, stood over Beauchamp, and fired five more times into his chest. He heard a scurrying in the waiting area. He rushed over to his filing cabinet and took out a second handgun wrapped in a towel. Careful not to touch the weapon directly, he placed it in Beauchamp's right hand and folded the large man's fingers around the handle and trigger.

Outside, he found the receptionist gone and the front door wide open. He drew a few deep breaths, then picked up the phone.

"911, what's your—"

"Help me," Jim cut her off, his voice booming and hysterical. "The man who killed my wife came to my office. He pulled a gun. I shot him. He isn't moving. Hurry. I'm begging you."

He hung up, pleased with his performance, and stood watching the blood pool around Beauchamp's head.

CHAPTER 19

KRISTINA HARING, JIM'S RECEPTIONIST, sat on the edge of the lobby's fountain, too distraught to feel the cold spray hitting the back of her neck.

"I'm dizzy," she told the plainclothes officer. "It's like I'm fighting for every breath."

"Just take it nice and easy, ma'am," the officer instructed. "The incident is over. You're safe now."

"The incident?" she repeated. "Forgetting your wallet at the supermarket is an incident. A shootout at work is...I don't know what it is."

The officer pressed on.

"How many shots did you hear?" he asked.

She shut her eyes, tried again to suck in a deep breath.

"First there were two," she said. "I ducked down behind my desk. Then I don't know how many I heard. They came one on top of the other. I must have run. I don't even remember how I got down here."

"Have you talked to Mr. Hood since?"

"No. I assumed . . . I figured he was . . ."

"Did you know he kept a gun in his office?"

"I had no idea. This is last thing I ever expected. Jim's clients are all . . ."

"Rich?"

"Upstanding. And it's not like this is a cash business. I just can't imagine why anyone would target Jim. The man's been through so much."

"How would you describe Mr. Hood?" the officer asked.

"What do you mean?"

"Does he have a temper? Have you ever seen him blow up at someone? At you?"

"My god, no. I can't even imagine it. He's the most even-keeled person I've ever met. There are times I wish he'd show a little more emotion."

"Are you saying he's cold?"

"No, I'm not saying that. But he's always in control of himself. At least at work he is."

"And you weren't able to hear any of their conversation before the shooting started?"

"No, but there couldn't have been much talk. He'd only been in there a minute. Maybe not even."

* * *

"Have you had any other contact with Mr. Beauchamp since the trial?" Detective Kyle Davis, a fifteen-year veteran of Homicide, asked Jim.

"No, none," Jim said.

"Not even by phone?" Detective Paul Greene, Davis's rookie partner, asked.

Jim shook his head. They were standing in the hall outside his office while forensics pored over the crime scene. Jim's eyes were red around the rims, and he seemed to be marching in place, as though his body had become one long twitch.

"And he had no feud with your family?" Davis asked.

"I'm telling you, I never saw him before today."

"So he just showed up here with a gun after he'd been acquitted of murdering your wife?" Greene asked.

"My god," Jim said, as though he hadn't heard the question, "I killed a man."

He pressed his back against a wall, struck himself hard in the forehead with an open palm, and kept hitting himself until Davis grabbed his wrists.

"Why don't you take time to gather yourself?" Davis said. "Go home and lie down for a bit. We'll talk later."

"All right," Jim said, blinking furiously and staring at the floor. "I guess I'll do that."

"I can have someone drive you if you want," Davis offered.

"No, I'll be okay," Jim said.

The detectives watched him scuffle off toward the elevator. Greene, puzzled, turned to Davis.

"You bought that performance?" he asked.

"I'm not sure," Davis said.

"Shouldn't we keep pressing him? Isn't he more likely to slip up now, before he's had time to think?"

"Maybe, but you can't catch someone in a lie if you don't know the truth. Let's gather the facts before we do anything else."

Greene followed Davis into Jim's office. There were lab techs bustling about, dusting the walls and furniture, gathering fibers from the carpet. The detectives stood over Beauchamp, examining his wounds, taking notes on the position of his body.

"I guess it could be self-defense," Greene said.

"How do you figure?" Davis asked.

"Beauchamp pulls a gun, but Hood is faster," Greene began. "He fires twice from behind his desk. Beauchamp staggers but doesn't go down. He's a big guy. He raises his gun again. Hood fires and keeps firing until Beauchamp falls."

"It's a possibility," Davis said. "Just not a very likely one."

"Why not?"

"Two reasons. First, Beauchamp, the career criminal who's almost definitely killed before, is the one who walks into the room and pulls a gun, but he doesn't get off a single shot? While Hood, the real estate geek with no priors, manages to empty his weapon? Doesn't smell right."

"Doesn't mean it's impossible."

"No, it doesn't."

"What's your second reason?"

"In all the years I've been doing this, I've never seen a gunshot victim fall straight back without having his weapon knocked from his hand."

"Beauchamp is a big man."

"I've seen them all sizes. Beauchamp would be the first, and I'm suspicious of firsts."

Greene thought it over.

"Okay," he said, "so maybe self-defense is a reach."

"A pretty far reach," Davis agreed. "But that doesn't make the case a slam dunk. There were two people in this room, and only one knows what really happened. And he's about to hire some very expensive lawyers."

CHAPTER 20

DAVIS AND GREENE DROVE north to break the news to Sharon Beauchamp, the victim's widow. Neither detective was surprised to find her at home in the middle of the afternoon. Sharon was only forty-five, but drug use and decades of hard living and poor nutrition had yellowed her teeth and shriveled her skin. She came to the door wearing ripped leggings and a long gray sweatshirt. The cigarette in her mouth was mostly ash.

Davis held up his badge.

"We're here about your husband," he said.

"Who else would you be here about?"

She waved them in, cleared coupon flyers and magazines and a dirty breakfast bowl from the couch, then gestured for them to sit. She dropped into a hard-backed chair, took one look at their faces and said: "He's dead, ain't he?"

Greene, caught off-guard by her matter-of-fact tone, let Davis take the lead.

"If you mean your husband," the senior detective said, "then yes, he is."

Sharon lit a new cigarette with the butt of the old one. Any object left lying around served as an ashtray: empty cans, the sole of a worn-out shoe, a cereal bowl, a coffee mug. The trailer smelled like its windows hadn't been opened in months. Greene wanted to take the conversation outside, but he knew Sharon would be less likely to cooperate with neighbors watching.

"That's who I mean," she said. "I had a bad feeling this morning. I told him not to go."

"Told him not to go where?" Davis asked, curious to see how much he could tease out of her before she started asking questions of her own.

"Where I'm guessing you found him," she said. "In that prick's office. Or somewhere nearby."

"Which prick would that be, ma'am?"

"Call me Sharon. I was already feelin' old. Now I'm a widow to boot."

"Sharon," Davis corrected. "Who was it your husband had gone to see?"

"I'm guessing you know that already, but I understand why you gotta ask. His name's Hood. Jim Hood. And he played my husband for a big fat fool."

"How's that?"

Davis kept his questions deliberately short: Sharon was off and running on her own, and he didn't want to slow her down. Greene took mental notes.

"Look, I know what it is you want to know, so I'll just

come out and give you everything I got. Hood said he'd pay Bruce to kill his wife. Twenty-five grand up front, plus another twenty-five once it was done. Well, it was done. Bruce nearly went away for it, and he kept his mouth shut about Hood all through the trial. That deserves a bonus if you ask me, but Bruce never even saw that second payment. He went there today to get it."

Greene fought to keep his jaw from dropping. Sharon didn't seem to realize she'd confessed to multiple felonies, from withholding information about a crime to aiding and abetting a murderer, though it would be nearly impossible to make any charge stick since her husband had been acquitted.

"Your husband told you all of this?" Davis asked.

"He more than told me: I saw that first twenty-five. Of course it's all gone now, and I don't got a thing to show for it. Hell, I still got two payments to make on this sorry-ass trailer. We were supposed to put that money towards a real house. Not that I believed it would ever happen. This sardine can'll be my tomb."

Her voice was nonchalant, as though she were complaining about a slight hike in the price of gasoline.

"How did your husband come to know Hood?" Davis asked.

"Bruce did some work for him a while back. Legit work, on one of his properties."

"How long ago was this?"

"Maybe ten years back. Bruce had just gotten out. Again. Jim looked like a real hero then, giving an ex-con a second chance when no one else would. He probably hired Bruce *because* he was an ex-con."

"Do you know if your husband ever did any other side jobs for Hood?" Davis asked.

"He did some moving-man work for a couple of Jim's clients. Nothing against the law."

Davis looked around at the duct-taped furniture and the stacks of trash. He knew the answer to his next question before he asked it.

"You wouldn't happen to have any paperwork showing that your husband worked for Jim Hood? Pay stubs, maybe?"

"He paid Bruce under the table. A blank envelope filled with cash every Friday. Maybe you can get the son-of-a-bitch on tax evasion, the way they did with Al Capone."

"We'll look into it," Davis said. "Do you know if Bruce had any friends who also worked for Hood?"

"You mean like to corroborate?"

Davis nodded.

"Bruce was a loner. Kept to himself on legit jobs and was strictly solo in the criminal world."

"Do you know if he did any other contract work?"

"You mean killings?"

Davis nodded again. Sharon blew out a deep lungful of smoke.

"Ha!" she said. "If he did, I'd be sampling cocktails on a beach somewhere. He did plenty of strong-arm stuff, though. Broke more bones than a schoolyard swing set. Usually for pocket change."

Davis leaned forward, made his voice soft and gentle.

"I hope this isn't indelicate," he said, "but you don't seem very broken up."

She shrugged.

"I guess I could sense the end coming. For both of us. Thirty years of chasing a high'll do that. I won't be far behind now. I just hope I make it to testify against Hood."

* * *

"Doesn't seem like she's hiding anything," Greene said, sliding behind the wheel.

"Yeah," Davis said, "but what kind of a witness will she make? She's an aging junkie who married a killer and probably has a rap sheet as long as his."

Greene turned the ignition, tapped his horn to scare off a flock of pigeons who were pecking at breadcrumbs in the gravel behind their car.

"So what's our next move?" he asked.

"We use what she gave us against Hood. Invite him down to the station as a witness and then hit him with what we know."

"Won't he just demand a lawyer?"

"Maybe. But a guy like that probably thinks he's about a thousand times smarter than a couple of glorified civil servants. We might get lucky."

"I'll make the call," Greene said.

CHAPTER 21

DAVIS SAT ALONE WITH Jim in an interrogation room while Greene watched through the two-way mirror.

"You see," Davis said, "we know that Beauchamp used to work for you. He was fresh out of prison when you hired him on one of your construction sites."

"So?" Jim asked.

Davis flashed a quizzical look.

"So you never mentioned that before. Not to us. Not when he was on trial for killing your wife. You claimed you'd never laid eyes on him."

"I hire a lot of people. Most of them are day workers. If Beauchamp did work for me, I have no memory of it."

Davis leaned back, folded hands behind his head and smiled.

"You know," he said, "my hardest day as a parent came when my son learned the word 'coincidence.' He was seven, maybe eight. He thought he'd discovered the world's secret free pass. Suddenly everything was a coincidence. When the dog vomited all over our carpet and we found an empty box of dog treats under my son's bed, that was a coincidence. When a trash can in our backyard caught fire the day my silver lighter went missing, that was a coincidence."

"Fascinating," Jim said. "Look, I've been here going on three hours. If you have a question to ask me, then—"

"My question is this," Davis said. "Was I wrong to punish my son for overfeeding our dog? For setting a fire in our yard? I mean, all I had to go on were a couple of coincidences."

Jim saw where the detective was headed.

"No," he said, "you weren't wrong."

"So I shouldn't have taken my son at his word?"

"Are you comparing me to an eight-year-old child?"

"If I were, I'd have to say his lies were more convincing."

Jim wouldn't rattle.

"There are some key differences," he said. "First, if Bruce Beauchamp worked for me and then killed my wife, I wouldn't call that a coincidence. Maybe he saw her at one of the job sites. Maybe he developed an obsession. Or maybe his obsession was with me. Beauchamp had nothing. It must have seemed to him like I had everything. Maybe he couldn't let that stand."

"Interesting theory," Davis said.

"And then, even if Beauchamp did work for me, it's not like we kept in touch. I wouldn't have seen him in over a decade. That's longer than your kid had been alive when the dog got sick. Do you know how many people have come and gone on my job sites over the last ten years? Why *would* I remember him?"

Davis started to giggle.

"That's funny?" Jim asked.

"I guess you're just too damn clever for your own good," Davis said. "I never mentioned how long ago Beauchamp worked for you. But you're right—it's been just over a decade. Is that another coincidence?"

Jim squirmed a little despite himself. Davis pressed on before his suspect had a chance to regroup.

"You know what I think," he said. "I think you hired Beauchamp to kill your wife."

"You've got an active imagination."

"Oh no, I don't have any imagination at all," Davis said. "What I have is a witness."

"A witness to what?"

"To an envelope stuffed with twenty-five thousand dollars. You were supposed to pay Beauchamp fifty grand, but you stiffed him on the second installment. I guess that could help your self-defense argument. He came to your office to demand his full payment. He had a gun, but you drew first. Of course, for that to work in court you'd have to admit to murdering your wife."

Jim gripped the edges of the table, raised up in his seat.

"I didn't kill Bonnie," he said. "You're going to take a drug addict's word—"

"I don't know what drug addict you're talking about," Davis interrupted. "What I do know is that Beauchamp earned that second twenty-five grand. He was facing life, and he didn't let out a peep about you. From where I sit, you're looking awfully ungrateful."

The last bit of Jim's patience snapped.

"Let's talk about where you sit," he said. "Let's talk about that bargain-rack suit you're wearing. Let's talk about the sad little middle-class upbringing I bet you gave that son of yours. You're right: you have no imagination. You carry a gun and send people to jail, but at the end of the day you're just another sad working stiff who couldn't think of anything better to do with his life."

Davis smiled.

"I hope you get a lot of self-made rich folk on your jury, because us working stiffs may not find you so sympathetic."

"Does that mean you're charging me?"

"I might as well. A confession would be nice, but I don't really need one. The DA's got a clear enough story to tell. You killed the killer to cover your tracks and save a few bucks."

"That's insane. I loved Bonnie."

"Once, maybe," Davis said. "But you were tired of her little mountain adventure. It was costing you money, and you had no intention of living up there, away from the action."

"That place wasn't costing me a thing," Jim said. "Bonnie was making a go of it."

"Please, Mr. Hood," Davis said. "We've been over the receipts. I believe 'hemorrhage' was the accountant's word. Then there's the fact that your marriage wasn't so strong to begin with. I mean, your wife was cheating on you with the handyman."

"Shut your—"

"Then there's the Widow Beauchamp, who, hard living aside, is about the most compelling witness I've come across. I'm a skeptic at heart, but she sold me within five minutes. You lured Beauchamp to your office thinking you could get rid of the last of the evidence and save a few bucks in the process. You should have just paid the man, Mr. Hood."

"All you've got is speculation," Jim said.

"Not true, Mr. Hood. There's physical evidence, too."

"What physical evidence?"

Davis considered whether or not to share. It was risky, but the more he piled on, the more likely Hood would be to panic.

"Bruce Beauchamp was left-handed," he said.

Jim looked confused.

"So?" he asked.

"So we found the gun in his right hand. And there wasn't a speck of blood on that gun."

"You could explain that a thousand different ways," Jim said.

"No, Mr. Hood, you couldn't," Davis said. "There's no way Beauchamp was holding a gun on you when you pumped five bullets into his chest. It's just not possible. I'll give you this, though: you put on a hell of a show for the 911 operator. You sure you don't want to do some more acting? Say how sorry you are? Shed a few tears? That kind of thing goes over big at sentencing."

Jim held up his hands.

"I want my lawyer," he said. "Now."

CHAPTER 22

JIM'S IN-LAWS WERE back in court for the trial, dressed to the nines and sitting in the front row. Jim could feel their eyes boring into the back of his skull; he imagined Bonnie's mother smiling each time the DA scored a victory. And for the prosecution, the victories kept coming.

Forensic experts supported Davis's theory of the crime scene: whether or not Beauchamp was left-handed, the impact of his fall would have knocked the gun from his hand, and the gun itself would have been spattered with blood.

A forensic accountant testified that Camp Nelson was a "money pit," costing the Hoods hundreds of thousands of dollars, a loss Jim would have recuperated through his wife's $500,000 insurance policy. He further testified that Jim's own real-estate holdings were spread so thin that he was more paper tiger than tycoon: "If things were to continue as they are now," the accountant told the DA, "he'd be bankrupt in a year."

Jim's team of celebrity attorneys couldn't stem the tide: it took the jury just under three hours to convict.

* * *

At sentencing, Jim was led into the courtroom in shackles and an orange jumpsuit. He scanned the front row and found Bonnie's parents in their usual place.

They'd left Mindy and Jim Jr. at home, just as they always did: why risk painting Jim as the single father of two bereft children when there was a good chance he'd go away for life?

The judge, a sixty-something man with slicked-back hair and glasses that looked more like goggles, called the session to order, then read a few preliminary remarks before asking Jim if he'd like to address the court. Jim stood and looked around the room. He forced himself to make eye contact with Bonnie's mother, then turned to face the judge.

"I just want to say how truly sorry I am," he began.

He'd rehearsed the speech in his cell, the way he'd rehearsed his 911 call in front of the bathroom mirror at home. But he hadn't made that call in front of an audience. Here, in the courtroom, he was keenly aware of all the people staring at him, rooting for him to fail.

"I shot Mr. Beauchamp in self-defense," he continued, "but if I could take it back, I would. Whatever the circumstances, I killed a man, and I'll have to live with that for the rest of my life."

It was like he was standing outside of himself, watching and critiquing his own performance. He was wooden, unconvincing. His voice rose and fell in all the wrong places. He'd practiced crying, but now the tears wouldn't come. And now that he'd stopped talking, he couldn't seem to start up again. He'd planned to give an outpouring of remorse, to throw himself at the judge's mercy, to beg for the Widow Beauchamp's forgiveness, but instead of pushing on he simply sat back down and hung his head.

The judge, unimpressed, sentenced him to twenty-nine years. The courtroom erupted in tears and applause. Jim kept his eyes on the ground as the bailiff led him away.

* * *

It was a long three months before Bonnie's father brought Mindy and Jim Jr. for a visit. Jim sat on one side of a thick glass wall, the kids on the other. They spoke through headsets. Mindy, Jim's tomboy, now wore a bright pink dress with a matching ribbon in her hair. Jim Jr. was suffering his first outbreak of acne. Both children put their hands up to the glass. Jim's father-in-law stood back beside one of the correctional officers. He hadn't so much as nodded to Jim.

"I wish I could bring you real clothes," Mindy told her father.

"This outfit is plenty comfortable," Jim said. "It's like wearing pajamas all the time."

Looking at them now, he regretted every harsh word, every instance when he'd lost his temper or refused to play one of Jim Jr.'s board games. More and more he wondered why he'd fought so hard against Bonnie's version of the future. A quiet country life spent watching his kids grow up . . . what else had he wanted?

"You look bigger, Daddy," Jim Jr. said. "I bet everyone here is afraid of you."

Jim smiled.

"It's not muscle," he said. "It's all the delicious meals they've been feeding me."

In fact, prison food had put a good twenty pounds on him. His face was bloated, and for the first time in his life his gut jutted out over his waistband.

"We saw you on the news," Mindy said.

Jim winced. He'd hoped his in-laws would shield the kids from media coverage. There was a difference between knowing the truth and being slapped with it day in and day out.

"I guess I'm famous now," he smiled.

"It isn't true, is it?" Mindy asked.

"What isn't true, honey?"

He regretted the question almost before he'd finished asking it. Better, he thought, to issue a blanket denial: *No sweetie, none of it is true. Even the police make mistakes.*

"They said that you didn't really have any money and that you hired that man to shoot Mommy and then you shot him because you couldn't afford to pay him," Jim Jr. blurted out.

Jim fought off a sharp pang in his gut.

"No," he said. "I didn't do any of those things. Your father's innocent."

But looking through the glass at his children, he accepted for the first time that he wasn't innocent. He'd spent his months in prison scheming, denying, searching for a way out. But there was no point in struggling: he was exactly where he belonged. His children would have better lives without him.

EPILOGUE

Two Years Later

"IT WILL TAKE AS much money to fix this place up as it will to buy it," Louise said.

"More, probably," Dan told her. "And a whole lot of labor."

"Still, it's a beautiful spot," she said.

"Can't argue that," he agreed.

They stood outside the boarded-up lodge, turning in slow circles as they studied the property. The balconies lining the second floor of the motel appeared to be hanging on by a thread, and the small cabins, also boarded up, were tagged with graffiti. Even the FOR SALE sign was in disrepair. Still, on a clear-blue day in autumn, with the sequoias towering above, there really was no denying the majesty of the place.

"Wasn't somebody murdered here?" Louise asked.

"I think so. I don't remember who or how, though," Dan said.

Louise shrugged.

"Well, I guess we might as well see the rest of it," she said. "There's supposed to be a stunning trail on the other side of that meadow."

They started across. The grass was thigh-high, and now and again one of them would stumble over an old car part or a discarded piece of furniture. When they reached the tree line, Louise turned back around for one more look.

"It's like a ghost town," she said. "Like something out of the Wild West."

And just as she said it, a shriveled little man wearing a torn plaid shirt and faded jeans emerged from the forest just a few yards away. He held a fishing pole in one hand and a tackle box in the other. His mostly gray hair, thinning up top, hung below his shoulders in the back. He wasn't old, but his shoulders were stooped and he seemed to have trouble walking.

"Howdy," he said, his expression none too friendly.

"Hi there," Dan answered.

"We aren't trespassing," Louise said, as though she anticipated a scolding. "We talked to the realtor, and—"

"Ah, you're investors," the man said.

"Something like that," Dan said.

Rudy looked the couple over. They were young, attractive. They had most of their adult lives ahead of them. He felt a wave of resentment.

"Well, you won't find anything better to do with your money," he said, forcing a grin.

"You think so?" Louise asked.

"I'm sure of it," Rudy said. "If I had the money, I'd buy the lodge myself. There's nowhere in the world like it."

Louise took another look over her shoulder.

"I think you're right," she said, locking arms with her husband. "I think this place has real potential."

THE ONE WHO KNOWS THE SECRETS IS THE ONE
WHO HOLDS THE POWER. CAN NYPD RED FIND THE
TRUTH BEFORE A CITY EXPLODES?

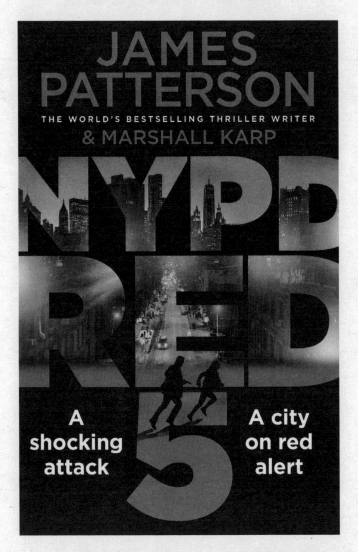

PLEASE TURN THE PAGE FOR A PREVIEW.

ONE

THERE WERE ONLY four words beneath the tattoo of the Grim Reaper on Aubrey Davenport's inner left thigh. But they spoke volumes.

Death is my aphrodisiac

And nowhere in the entire city was her libido more on point than at the Renwick Smallpox Hospital, a crumbling three-story, U-shaped monster on the southern tip of Roosevelt Island.

Once a marvel of neo-Gothic architecture, Renwick was now a rotting stone carcass, the final way station for thirteen thousand men, women, and children who had died a painful death.

For the city fathers, Renwick was a historical landmark. For the urban explorers, it was New York's most haunted house. But for Aubrey Davenport, it was a sexual Mecca, and on a warm evening in early May, she and a willing partner scaled the eight-foot fence, made their way into the bowels of the moldering labyrinth, and spread a thick quilted blanket on the rocky floor.

She kicked off her shoes, removed her shirt and bra, shucked her jeans, and stood there, naked except for a pair of aquamarine bikini panties.

Her nipples responded to the caress of a cool breeze that drifted over her breasts, and she inhaled the earthy scent of the decay around her, mixed with the dank overtones of river water.

She dropped to her knees on the blanket, closed her eyes, and waited for her partner.

She shuddered as he silently slipped the noose around her neck. His fingers were long and slender. *Piano player fingers,* her mother used to call them. *Like your father has.*

As a child, Aubrey wondered why a man blessed with the hands of a concert pianist never played an instrument, never even cared to. But somewhere along the way she came to understand that Cyril Davenport's long, slender fingers made music of another kind: the crescendo of sound that came from her parents' bedroom on a nightly basis.

Aubrey felt the rope pull tighter. Rope was a misnomer. It was a long strand of silk—the belt from a robe, perhaps—and it felt soft and smooth as he cinched it against her carotid arteries.

He took her shoulders and guided her body to the ground until her belly was flat against the cotton blanket below her.

"Comfy?" he asked.

She laughed. *Comfy* was such a dumb word.

"You're laughing," he said. "Life is good, yes?"

"Mmmmmm," she responded.

"It's about to get better," he said, tugging at the waist-band of her panties and sliding them down to her ankles. His fingers teased as they walked slowly up her leg and came to rest on the patch of ink etched into her thigh. His thumb stroked the shrouded figure and arced along the scythe that was clutched in its bony claw.

"Hello, death," he said, removing his hand.

Crack! The cat-o'-nine-tails lashed across her bare bottom, burning, stinging, each individual knotted-leather strap leaving its mark. She bit down hard and buried a scream into the blanket.

Pain was the appetizer. Pleasure was the main course. Her body tensed as she waited for his next move.

In a single, practiced motion he bent her legs at the knees, tipped them back toward her head, grabbed the tether that was around her neck, and tied the other end to her ankles.

"Hand," he ordered.

Aubrey, her right arm beneath her stomach, reached all the way down until her hand was between her legs.

"Life is good," he repeated. "Make it better."

Her fingers groped, parting the pleats, entering the canal, tantalizing the nerve endings. The effect was dizzying: the man with the whip, the foul-smelling ruins, and the inescapable presence of thirteen thousand dead souls.

He said something, but she couldn't hear over the sound of her own labored breathing. And then—the point of no return. She felt the swell of gratification surging through her body, and with near surgical precision she gently lowered her feet toward the ground.

The silk rope around her neck tightened, compressing her carotid arteries. The sudden loss of oxygen along with the buildup of carbon dioxide made her light-headed, giddy, almost hallucinogenic. The orgasm came in waves. It left her gasping for air, but the euphoria was so powerful, so addictive, that she intensified the pressure around her neck, knowing she could go just a few more seconds.

If erotic asphyxiation were an Olympic event, Aubrey Davenport would have been a world-class contender. Her brain was just on the threshold of losing consciousness when she released the death grip, and brought her feet back toward her buttocks.

But the noose refused to relax. If anything, it felt tighter. Panic seized her. She thrashed, pulled her hands up to her throat, and clawed at the silk, fighting for air and finding none.

She never made mistakes. Something must have snagged. She reached behind her neck, desperately trying to find some slack, when her fingers found his hand. He jerked hard on the silk cord, and her arms flailed.

She slumped, too weak to struggle, all hope gone. Everything went black, and as the reaper stepped out of the darkness to claim her, tears streamed down her cheeks, because in the last seconds of her life, Aubrey Davenport finally realized that she didn't want to die.

TWO

THE COTILLION ROOM at The Pierre hotel bubbled over with New York's wealthiest—including a few who were wealthier than some countries.

They were the richest of the rich, the ones who get invited to fifty-thousand-dollars-a-plate dinners when one of their own wants to tap them for a worthy cause. In this case, the charity with its hand out was the Silver Bullet Foundation.

The thirty-foot-long banner at the front of the hall proclaimed its noble mission: FIGHTING FOR THE LESS FORTUNATE.

The man in the black tie and white jacket busing tables in the rear had boiled when he first saw the sign. *They haven't done shit for me, and I'm the least fortunate person in the room.*

They're like swans, he thought as he watched them glide serenely from table to table: *so elegant, so regal, but fiercely territorial and vicious when they feel threatened. And like swans,* he observed, *they are oh so white.*

He counted half a dozen black swans among them, but for the most part, the people of color were there to serve. He fit right in.

With his shoulders slumped, his jaw slack, and a cheap pair of clear-lens nerd glasses to dial down the intensity of his piercing black eyes, he was practically invisible, and definitely forgettable.

The only human contact he'd had in the three hours since donning the uniform was with a besotted old patrician who'd slurred, "Hey fella, where's the men's room?"

Shortly after nine, the lights dimmed, the chatter died down, and the commanding voice of James Earl Jones piped through the sound system.

"Ladies and gentlemen, please welcome the cofounder and chairman of the Silver Bullet Foundation, Mr. Princeton Wells."

The staff had been instructed to stop work during the presentation, and the busboy dutifully stepped into the shadows near a fire exit as Princeton Wells bounded onto the stage.

Wells was his typically charming, still-boyish-at-forty, old-moneyed self. And lest any man in the room suspect that someone that rich and that good-looking wasn't getting laid, Wells kicked off the festivities by introducing his current girlfriend, Kenda Whithouse, to a captive audience.

Ms. Whithouse stood up, waved to the room, and threw

her billionaire boyfriend a kiss. She was only twenty-three, an actress who was not quite yet tabloid fodder, but who clearly had the talent to fill out an evening gown. Those who knew Princeton Wells had no doubt that the gown would be lying crumpled on his bedroom floor by morning.

Having trotted out his latest eye candy, Wells got down to the serious business of reminding all the do-gooders in the room how much good they were doing for the city's less fortunate.

"And no one," he decreed, "has been more supportive of Silver Bullet than Her Honor, the mayor of New York, Muriel Sykes."

The city's first female mayor, her approval rating still sky-high after only four months in office, was greeted by enthusiastic applause as she stepped up to the podium.

The busboy did not applaud. He slid his smartphone from his jacket pocket and tapped six digits onto the keypad.

One, two, two, nine, nine, seven.

He stared at it, not seeing a sequence of numbers but a moment in time that had changed his life forever: December 29, 1997. His finger hovered over the Send button as the mayor began to speak.

"I'm not a big fan of giving speeches at rubber chicken dinners," she said, "even when the chicken turns out to be grade A5 Miyazaki Wagyu beef."

Everyone but the busboy found that funny.

"On the second day of my administration, I had a

meeting with the four founders of Silver Bullet. They showed me a picture of an abandoned old warehouse in the Bronx, and I said, 'Who owns that eyesore?' And they said, 'You do, Madam Mayor. But if you sell it to us for a dollar, we will raise enough money to convert it into permanent housing for a hundred and twenty-five chronically homeless adults.'

"I accepted their offer, framed the dollar, and am thrilled to announce that next month we will start construction. I'm here tonight to thank you all for your generous contributions and to introduce one of the four men who spearheaded this project. He is the brilliant architect whose vision will turn that dilapidated monstrosity into a beautiful apartment complex for some of our neediest citizens. Ladies and gentlemen, please welcome Del Fairfax."

Fairfax, architect to the one percent, stepped onto the stage to show off what wonders he could create for the indigent. Spot-on handsome and aw-shucks personable, he rested a laptop on the podium, flipped it open, and said, "I know how fond you all are of PowerPoint presentations, so I put one together for you. Only ninety-seven slides."

The half-sloshed crowd warmly gave him his due.

"Just kidding," he said. "Princeton told me if I showed more than five, you'd start asking for your money back. The new facility will be called Tremont Gardens. First, let me show you what it looks like now."

He picked up a wireless remote and pushed a button.

The explosion rocked the Cotillion Room.

CHAPTER 1

KYLIE AND I had never been attached to Mayor Sykes's security detail before, but once she agreed to speak at the Silver Bullet Foundation fund-raiser, she recruited us for the night.

The word came down from our boss. "The mayor wants to do a little fund-raising of her own," Captain Cates said. "She comes up for reelection in three and a half years, and as long as she's going to spend the evening rubbing elbows with her biggest donors, she wants to assure them that she's not just a champion of the unfortunate poor. She cares deeply about the disgustingly rich. And what better way to demonstrate her concern for their welfare than by trotting out a couple of poster cops from NYPD Red?"

"Thanks, but no thanks," Kylie said. "Doesn't she realize we already spend sixty hours a week overprotecting the overprivileged? Now she's inviting us to suck up to them at some—"

Cates cut her off. "Did I use the word *invite?* Because

the last time I read the department manual I didn't see anything about *invitations* being passed down the chain of command. The mayor specifically instructed me to assign Detectives Kylie MacDonald and Zach Jordan to her security detail. Consider yourselves assigned. No RSVP required."

I figured it would be the most boring night of the week. And I was right—until the podium exploded.

It was one of those shock and awe explosions. The blinding flash, the deafening boom, the thick smoke, the chemical stench, and the flying chunks of wood, glass, metal, and Del Fairfax.

Mayor Sykes had just come off the stage and returned to her seat when the bomb went off. Kylie and I were only an arm's length away from her. We yanked her from her chair and, shielding her body with ours, bulled our way through the chaos toward our prearranged exit door.

At least fifty other frenzied people had the same idea.

I keyed my radio and yelled over the din, "Explorer, this is Red One. Vanguard is safe. Egress Alpha is blocked. We're making our way toward Bravo."

We did a one-eighty and shoved the mayor toward the kitchen. The path was clear, and the vast stainless steel hub of the hotel's multimillion-dollar banquet business was almost deserted. Except for a few stragglers, the staff had beaten a quick retreat through a rear fire door and down a stairwell to the employee locker rooms.

At that point, many of them decided that they were out of harm's way, and at least twenty of them were standing in the corridor, almost every one with a cell phone to his or her ear.

"NYPD. Get out of the way! Get out of the fucking way!" Kylie bellowed as we elbowed our way through the log-jam.

A hotel security guard saw us coming and pushed open a metal door that led to the outside world. As soon as she felt the cool night air and heard the sounds of her city, the mayor stopped.

"Please," she said. "I'm too old for this shit. Let me catch my breath."

"Sorry, ma'am," Kylie said. "Not here. We only have an-other hundred feet. Keep going, or Zach and I will carry you to the car."

The mayor gave Kylie an enigmatic stare that could have been anywhere on the spectrum from contempt to gratitude.

"Nobody…" she said, breathing heavily, "carries… Muriel Sykes…anywhere. Lead the way."

We single-filed down a narrow alleyway, past a row of Dumpsters, and I radioed ahead to her team.

The alley came out on East 61st Street between Madison and Fifth Avenues. Just as we got to the far end, the mayor's black SUV drove up onto the sidewalk. Her driver, Charlie, jumped out and swung open the rear door. I of-fered to help the mayor into the back seat, but she waved me off.

"This is as far as I'm going," she said.

"Ma'am, this is not the place for you to be," Kylie said.

"A maniac just set off a bomb in my city, Detective. This is *my* responsibility."

"Yes, ma'am, but maniacs have a bad habit of setting off secondary bombs targeting people who have just run from the first," Kylie said. "And it's our responsibility to get you to safe ground."

"Madam Mayor," Charlie said, "they're setting up a command center at the Park Avenue Armory. I can have you there in two minutes."

Crisis averted. The mayor got in the car, shut the door, and rolled down her window. "Thank you, Detectives," she said. That was it. Three words, and the window went back up.

Within seconds, the oversize, bulletproof Ford Explorer peeled out and, with lights flashing and sirens wailing, whisked Muriel Sykes away to the longest night of her fledgling administration.

"I hate these boring babysitting jobs," Kylie said. "Let's go do some real police work."

The two of us ran back down the alley and up the stairs toward the smoke-filled ballroom.

CHAPTER 2

KYLIE AND I joined the influx of first responders who raced to help the injured. It was just cops and firefighters at first, but when a bomb explodes in a public place, it sets off a Pavlovian response. Law enforcement agencies everywhere start salivating.

By the ten o'clock news cycle, The Pierre was the most famous crime scene in America, and everyone—Feds, staties, NYPD, FDNY, even the DEA—wanted a piece of the action.

Fortunately, the turf war dust settled long before the acrid gray cloud in the Cotillion Room, and Kylie and I were thrown together with Howard Malley, an FBI bomb tech we'd run into before.

Malley is a hawkeyed post-blast investigator and a pull-no-punches New York ballbuster, but he can also get testy as a cobra when you disagree with him. In short, he was a lot like Kylie. Maybe that's why I liked him.

The two of us suited up—disposable Tyvek coveralls,

sock boots, face mask—and we crossed the threshold to ground zero. The rear of the room was remarkably intact. Flower arrangements and wineglasses were still sitting on several tables, waiting to be cleared.

We walked toward the spot where Del Fairfax, Princeton Wells, and Mayor Sykes had stood less than an hour ago, wooing their wealthy benefactors. Windows were shattered, wood-paneled walls were peppered with shrapnel, and the floor was littered with the detritus of the blast: scorched drapery, sparkling chunks of chandelier crystal, overturned chairs, silverware, shoes, purses—thousands of puzzle pieces that had made a picture-perfect evening and now lay in tatters, covered in thick dust and splattered with blood.

At the center of it all was the man who was supposed to make sense of this seemingly senseless act. He was squatting at one end of the forty-foot charred swath that had been the stage. Agent Malley, a bald-headed, gray-bearded FBI lifer, was squinting at a pair of forceps in his right hand through a pocket magnifying glass. He looked up when he heard us coming his way. "Well, if it isn't Jordan and MacDonald," he said. "How's business at NYPD's Fat Cat Squad?"

"Booming," Kylie deadpanned. "You find something down there?"

"Maybe." He stood up. "If you think of this mess as a four-thousand-square-foot haystack, I may have just found a needle. Take a look."

Kylie and I took turns studying the prize dangling from

Malley's stainless steel pincers. It was a piece of wire. Three pieces, actually—one red, one white, one blue— twisted together in pigtail fashion. It was as thin as a strand of angel-hair pasta and no more than two inches long.

"And that's significant?" I asked.

"Again, maybe. These bomb makers—we see them as mass murderers, but they like to think of themselves as artists." He gave the word a French spin so that it came out *arteests*.

"And like artists everywhere, they are compelled to sign their masterpieces. This little red, white, and blue twisty thing isn't something I've come across before, so the thought popped into my head that maybe it's our bomber's signature."

"Red, white, and blue," Kylie said. "So what does that mean—death to America?"

"The bomb says death. I think the wire is about the guy who built it."

"Red, white, and blue," Kylie repeated. "You think he's an American?"

"Or he could be a color-blind Lithuanian. It would be nice to know what it symbolizes, but what would be really helpful is if this is his trademark, and he's in our global database. I'll take it back to the office and see if we get a hit."

"So, what's your take so far?" I asked.

He bagged the tiny fragment of wire, marked it, and put it in an evidence bin. "It wasn't a terrorist attack," he said.

"You sure?"

"Hell, no. I'm just a humble underpaid government employee, not Harry Potter. But you asked what's *my take*, which kind of means my educated guess after snooping around for twenty minutes. It'll never stand up in court, but right now my take is that with only one dead and twenty-two injured, this is not the handiwork of a dyed-in-the-wool, trained-in-Syria jihadi."

"Not a terrorist?" Kylie said. "Howard, this guy took out twenty-three people with a bomb."

"You're not listening, Detective," Malley said, his defense mechanisms going on point. "I didn't say he wasn't a pro. This guy is top-shelf. But he was using a shaped charge aimed at killing one person. Those twenty-two other people were collateral damage, some from the blowback, but mostly from the stampede. I don't know nearly as much about dealing with zillionaires as you do, but I'm guessing this was an every-man-for-himself crowd. They'd have a lot fewer broken bones if they didn't panic. This guy was only after Fairfax. It wasn't terrorism. It was personal."

"If it were personal," Kylie said, "wouldn't it have been easier just to murder him in his bed?"

Malley shrugged. "I'm guessing he wanted to make a public statement. I just have no idea what he was trying to say." He winked. "But then, that's not my problem."

CHAPTER 3

MALLEY WAS RIGHT. Terrorism was Homeland's problem, but homicide—especially an A-list victim like Del Fairfax—was all ours.

Other than being witness to the final seconds of his life, we knew nothing about him. We needed to talk to someone who did. We tracked down Princeton Wells. He was still at the hotel, only he'd relocated to the thirty-ninth floor.

"Anything I can do to help," he said, opening the door to a suite with sweeping views of Central Park.

He'd traded his formal wear for a pair of wrinkled khaki cargo shorts, a faded gray T-shirt, no shoes, no socks.

The mayor had introduced us to Wells earlier in the evening. We'd given him our cards, and he'd joked about hoping he'd never need them. Yet here we were, only hours later, following him into the living room.

"Grab a chair," he said, heading for a well-stocked wet bar. "Drink?"

We declined. He tossed some rocks into a glass and added four inches of Grey Goose. Then he uncorked a bottle of white and poured an equally generous amount into a crystal goblet.

He took a hit of vodka, set the wine on the coffee table in front of us, and said, "What have you got so far?"

"We're sorry for the loss of your friend," I said, "but the fact that he was the only one killed points to the possibility that he may have been the primary target."

"That's insane," Wells said. "Who would want to kill Del?"

"That's what Detective MacDonald and I are here to ask you. How well did you know him?"

"We've been best friends since high school. We roomed together in college. Twenty years ago we cofounded Silver Bullet along with Arnie Zimmer and Nathan Hirsch. Del and I were like brothers."

"Did he have any enemies? Anyone who would want to see him dead?"

"This is fucking surreal," he said, tipping the glass to his lips and draining it. "I need another drink." He padded back to the bar.

The last thing Princeton Wells needed was more alcohol, which is something I would have told him if he were an ordinary citizen, and I were an ordinary cop. But he was a billionaire many times over, and I was a detective first grade trained to deal with the privileged class, be they shit-faced or sober. I watched as he ignored the ice and replenished the vodka.

"This is a beautiful place," Kylie said, backing off the raw subject of his murdered best friend.

He smiled. "Thanks. I've had it for three years now. The view is spectacular when it snows. Point the remote at the fireplace, open a bottle of wine..."

"Did someone say *wine?*"

Kenda Whithouse entered the room, her hair wrapped in a towel, her body somewhat covered by a man's tuxedo shirt.

"Already poured," Wells said, pointing to the glass he'd left on the table.

She picked it up, sat on a sofa, and discreetly tucked her legs under her.

"Kenda," Wells said, "these detectives are from NYPD."

"Nice to meet you," she said. "Did you catch them yet?"

"We're working on it," I said.

"It was terrible. Like one of those disaster movies, only it was real. I was lucky I wasn't killed. Bad enough I got covered with all that crap flying through the air. I looked like one of those homeless women Princeton is building housing for. I had to wash my hair three times to get the smell out."

Wells sat down next to her, took another belt of the vodka, and shifted his body so he could square off with the two of us.

"You want to know what I think, Detectives? I think that bomb was meant for the mayor. I mean, she left the podium just a few seconds before it blew. That's the only thing that makes sense. There's always someone with a hard-on for politicians. But Del Fairfax? Everybody loved him. Hell, they love the four of us. We raise hundreds of millions of dollars. We provide food, shelter, and education for these people, but more important, we give them purpose, hope—"

He stopped, looked at the glass in his hand, and set it down. "Sorry. A couple of drinks and I go all humanitarian commando on you. My point is, nobody wants to kill the golden goose. Silver Bullet doesn't have enemies."

"What about Fairfax's personal life?" Kylie asked.

"Del was a player. Never married. And why would he? He was rich, he was good-looking, and the gals loved him."

"Did any of these *gals* have husbands?" Kylie asked.

"God, no. Del would never poach another man's wife. He was a hound, but he wasn't into drama."

My cell rang. It was Cates. I stepped into the foyer to take the call.

"Fill me in," she said.

"The blast investigator flat out said, 'It wasn't a terrorist attack.' He thinks it was a targeted hit at the victim. But Princeton Wells says the vic was a saint, beloved by all, so the bomb must have been meant for the mayor."

"I doubt it," Cates said. "Sykes was a last-minute addition to the program. This attack was planned, prepped— but I'll alert Gracie security. What else?"

"Nothing else, boss. There were four hundred people in the room, yours truly included, and we can't find a single witness who witnessed anything."

"How soon can you and MacDonald tear yourself away from the scene?"

"About twelve seconds. We're coming up dry here."

"Then get your asses out to Roosevelt Island. Chuck Dryden has a body he wants you to meet."

"Another homicide? For *Red*?"

"What can I tell you, Jordan?" Cates said. "It's a bad night for the rich and famous."

CHAPTER 4

"NEVER UNDERESTIMATE THE insanity of people with money," Kylie said.

"Did you just open a fortune cookie, or is this the beginning of a fascinating observation?" I asked.

We were in the car on our way to Roosevelt Island.

"I'm talking about Princeton Wells," she said. "Why in God's name would he buy a three-bedroom suite at The Pierre hotel when he owns a six-story town house on Central Park West less than a mile away? It's crazy."

"Why does Bruce Wayne dress up in a cape and a cowl and fight crime in Gotham City when he could just as easily sit back and have Alfred, the butler, wait on him hand and foot inside the stately Wayne Manor? Kylie, the rich have their own special brand of craziness."

"You'd think I'd have figured that out after working Red for almost a year, but when we called Wells, and he said he was on the thirty-ninth floor of the hotel, I automatically assumed he rented a room for the night."

"Guys like Wells don't rent rooms for the night," I said.

She grinned. "Just women. Poor thing had to wash her hair three times."

"I take it you don't approve of his choice."

"Just the opposite. She's perfect for the man who wants to devote his energy to being of service to the less fortunate."

I could tell by the glint in her eyes that she was just warming up, and she was ready to slice and dice Kenda Whithouse like a late-night comedian skewering the Kardashians. But her cell phone rang.

She checked the caller ID, smiled, and picked up. "Hey, babe, I didn't think you were going to call."

Babe? Personal call, I decided, my keen detective senses kicking in. I checked my watch and the look on Kylie's face: 11:47 p.m. Delighted. Very personal.

I couldn't hear the voice on the other end, but it went on for a solid minute. Finally, Kylie responded with, "Hey, you win some, you lose some."

A pause, and then she said, "I wish I could, but my partner and I just caught our second homicide of the night." A laugh, followed by, "Don't blame me. You're the one who thought it would be fun to date a cop. I'll talk to you tomorrow."

She hung up. "Damn it, Zach, these dead millionaires are killing my social life. I just had to turn down an invitation for drinks at Gansevoort PM."

She was baiting me, waiting for me to ask who she turned down.

Keep waiting. I'm not asking.

"I was there last week," she said. "The music is totally badass, but the bottle service prices in the Platinum Room are off the charts."

I refused to bite. I kept my eyes on the road and my mouth shut.

"Have you ever been to the Ganz?" she asked.

"Not yet," I said, "but if a dead body shows up, I'm there in a heartbeat."

That shut her up.

Normally, cops are happy to share the intimate details of their lives with their partners, but my relationship with Kylie was far from normal. We met a dozen years ago at the academy. She had just dumped her drug-addict boyfriend, and I turned out to be just what she needed to fill the void.

For twenty-eight days we couldn't keep our hands off each other. Somewhere along the way I fell in love with her. But on Day 29, the ex-boyfriend, Spence Harrington, came back, fresh out of rehab, begging her for one last chance. She gave it to him, and a year later they were married.

For the next ten years they were the perfect boldface couple. Kylie was a smart, beautiful, decorated NYPD detective, and Spence became one of New York's most prolific and successful TV writer-producers.

And then one day the drugs pulled him back in, and he began to spiral out of control. To her credit, Kylie did everything she could to save him from self-destructing, only to learn the hard way that you can't save an addict from himself.

Two months ago, Spence walked out on her, and when it was clear he wasn't coming back, Kylie slowly dipped her toe back into the dating pool.

There was a line of boys in blue hoping to get on her dance card, but she turned them all down.

"I'm not hooking up with any cops," she told me. "One was enough."

I didn't ask if that meant I had set the bar impossibly high or I'd ruined it for every other cop in the department.

For weeks she'd been dropping little hints about the new man in her life, egging me on to probe for details. But I was damned if I was going to ask.

All I knew for sure was that whoever this guy was, he could afford bottle service in the Platinum Room at the fucking Ganz.

I have no idea why he'd want to be surrounded by loud people and even louder music, and then spend thousands of dollars on a bottle of booze he could buy for fifty bucks at a liquor store.

But like Kylie said, "Never underestimate the insanity of people with money."

CHAPTER 5

ROOSEVELT ISLAND IS a two-mile strip of land in the East River. It's so narrow—barely eight hundred feet wide—that from the air it looks like a piece of dental floss in between two teeth called Manhattan and Queens.

Eleven thousand people live there. Most of the other eight and a half million New Yorkers have either never been or popped by once when they took the kids for a ride on the aerial tramway that connects the island to Manhattan.

I drove across the Ed Koch Bridge, made a U-turn in Queens, and then doubled back over a second bridge to Main Street on Roosevelt Island. The trip took twenty-seven minutes. The tram takes three.

We followed East Loop Road to the underdeveloped southern tip of the island, where there was a cluster of vehicles from various city agencies. One of them, an NYPD generator truck, lit up a gray stone hulk that looked like an abandoned medieval castle waiting for the wrecking ball.

"Good morning, Detectives," a familiar voice called out.

It was a few minutes after midnight, so technically it was morning. And nobody is more technical than our favorite anal-retentive, obsessive-compulsive crime scene investigator, Chuck Dryden.

"It's my first homicide in 10044," he said, walking toward us.

I smiled as I imagined him racing home after work to color in another section of his Zip Code Murder Map.

"What do you know about autoerotic asphyxia?" he asked.

"As much as I know about Russian roulette," Kylie said. "It's a game you can win a hundred times, but you can only lose once. Who's our victim?"

"Caucasian female, thirty-eight years old. Driver's license in her purse ID's her as Aubrey Davenport."

That explained the Red connection. Davenport was a documentarian whose films focused on social justice: the impact of oil spills, wrongful medical deaths, gun violence in America—the kind of polarizing journalism that gets some people to write their congressman and others to send her hate mail.

We made our way over the rocky ground to where she was lying facedown on a blanket. She was naked except for a pair of panties around her ankles. Her back was covered with welts, and she'd been trussed with several lengths of blue fabric, one end knotted around her neck, the other attached to her ankles. I've seen hundreds of dead bodies, but I was unnerved by the grotesqueness of this one.

"Was she sexually assaulted?" Kylie asked.

"No evidence of penetration," Dryden said. "No sign of a struggle. She cooperated with whoever tied her up. She was as much a volunteer as a victim."

"You telling me she signed on for this?" I said. "Whip-lashes and all?"

Dryden shook his head. "You have much to learn about sexually deviant behavior, grasshopper."

"All I know is what I heard from the missionaries. Feel free to enlighten me, sensei."

He cracked a smile, which for Chuck Dryden is the equivalent of a standing ovation. "AEA is for the most part a male sport—often people you'd never suspect. Family men, respected pillars of the community who get off by cheating death. They tie ropes around their neck and gen-itals, attach the other end to a pipe or a doorknob, and then masturbate, slowly lowering their bodies to cut off the oxygen to their brain, which I'm told gives them the best orgasm they've ever experienced…although some-times it's also their last.

"Most of the recorded deaths are people who do it solo, but this woman didn't want to take chances. She had a spotter, most likely a man. His role was to tie her up and to help her if anything went wrong. Her biggest mistake was trusting him. Look at this knot."

He pointed to a loop in the middle of the sash. "It's

supposed to be a slipknot, a fail-safe that she can pull at any time to set herself free. But he tied it so that instead of releasing, it tightened."

"A good lawyer will say it could have been an accident," Kylie said. "Not everyone has a merit badge in autoerotic knots."

"And that's exactly what the killer would like us to think," Dryden said. "But look at these ligature marks around her neck. If she had control over her oxygen flow, they would be on a downward angle toward her legs. But these are going in the opposite direction, and they're deep, which to me indicates he was standing over her, and pulling up hard. I'd like to see a lawyer talk his way out of that."

"What about the scratches on her throat?" I asked.

"Self-inflicted. She realized what the killer was doing, but it was too late. She didn't have the strength to put up a fight. Bottom line: Aubrey Davenport did not die because of kinky sex gone wrong. She was murdered."

"Thanks, Chuck," I said. "I'm looking forward to hearing you say those exact words in front of a jury. Who found the body?"

"A couple of fourteen-year-old boys with a twelve-pack who were planning a memorable evening and got more than they bargained for. They called it in at 9:36. Time of death is anywhere in the eight-hour window prior to that."

"What else was in her purse besides her ID?"

"Cash, credit cards, cell phone, a parking stub from a

garage in Brooklyn time-stamped 4:52 p.m., and a SIG Sauer P238, which she unfortunately didn't get to fire."

"Prints?"

"This place is too rocky for me to come up with any usable fingerprints, but I do have three very telling foot-prints."

"Can you get a cast? A shoe size?"

"They're not the kind of feet that wear shoes." Dryden smiled. He enjoyed leading us up to the mountaintop, especially when he was the one who discovered the mountain.

He shined his flashlight on three equidistant circles in the dust a few yards away from the body.

"There was a tripod there," he said. "Whoever killed her filmed it."

CHAPTER 6

IT'S GOTTEN EASIER for people to get away with murder in New York City.

While the brass at One P P are quick to promote the fact that homicides in our city are at historic lows, there's one statistic they don't like to talk about. In four out of every ten cases, the killer isn't caught.

Other cities with the same problem can blame it on the rise of drug and gang homicides. When drug dealers or gangbangers start killing, the neighborhood goes blind. No witnesses usually means no arrests.

But New York has a singular reason for our less-than-stellar batting average.

9/11.

When the towers fell, Ground Zero became the emotional focal point of our national tragedy. But for NYPD, it was the biggest crime scene in the city's history. That morning, 2,749 men, women, and children were murdered, and every homicide demanded our full attention—one victim at a time.

The task of bringing closure to thousands of families fell squarely on the shoulders of our most seasoned detectives. It was physically and emotionally draining police work, and within two years of the attacks, three thousand of our best investigators pulled their pins. They retired, and an additional eight hundred detectives were reassigned to the new counterterrorism unit.

That left a hole that has never been filled. To this day there are precinct detectives working everything from petty larceny to major felonies who have hundreds of unsolved crimes on their plates. They catch new cases faster than they can clear the old, and there's no one available to share the load.

That kind of clearance rate won't cut it at Red. So when we need backup, we get it. At 1:45, while Kylie and I were still combing the grounds of the Renwick Smallpox Hospital, I got a call from Danny Corcoran, a detective second grade working out of Manhattan North.

I knew Danny from the One Nine. He's smart, thorough, and gifted with a wicked sense of humor.

"Zach," he said, "I heard you need some grunt work on a homicide, and I just got the good news that I'm your designated grunt."

I gave him a quick overview and told him to secure Aubrey Davenport's apartment and office, in Manhattan, and her car, which was in a garage in Brooklyn.

"And I need a next of kin," I said. "Kylie and I will do the notification."

"I'm on it," he said. "By the by, I'm breaking in a new partner. Tommy Fischer."

"And?"

"He's got his pluses and his minuses."

"What are the minuses?" I asked.

"Lactose intolerant. On the plus side, he's a great kisser."

I hung up, laughing. I realized it was the first time I'd laughed since I followed the mayor into The Pierre six hours earlier, and it was a welcome release. Kylie and I were looking at two very ugly cases, and it felt good to know that I could count on Danny Corcoran to break the tension along the way.

He called back twenty minutes later.

"Your vic has an older sister, Claudia Davenport Moretti. She works in the financial aid office at Barnard College. Her husband, Nick Moretti, is an air traffic controller out of La Guardia. Two kids. No record, no drama. From what I can tell, they're as normal as bumps on a gherkin."

He gave me an address on West 74th Street in Manhattan.

Ten minutes later, Kylie and I were back in the car on our way to break the bad news. She drove. I curled up against the passenger door, closed my eyes, and drifted off to the hum of our tires on steel bridge plates.

My cell woke me up. It was Cheryl.

Dr. Cheryl Robinson is the forensic psychologist

attached to Red. Despite her predominantly Irish roots, she inherited the smoldering Latina looks of her Puerto Rican grandmother. When we met four years ago, Cheryl was married, so for me she was just another coworker who happened to be magnetically desirable, mind-numbingly beautiful, and totally unavailable.

Then she suddenly became an unmarried coworker, and I wasted no time trying to see if my fantasies could become a reality. Much to my amazement, they have. She's the first woman I've fallen in love with since Kylie, and I wake up every day hoping I don't torpedo my good fortune.

This was the fifth time she'd called me since the bomb went off at The Pierre. I picked up the phone.

"Don't you stalkers ever go to sleep?" I said.

"I was asleep," she said, "but I woke up, turned on the news, and they keep rerunning videos of the explosion. Zach, you could have been killed."

"But I wasn't. I'm fine. Just exhausted. Kylie and I are still out on the road."

"Call it a night, but don't go back to your apartment. Come over here. I need to give you a hug."

"We picked up a second case. We're on the way to no-tify the victim's family. Can I get a rain check on the hug?"

"You're in luck. My rain checks come with dinner and a sleepover. You interested?"

"I said I was exhausted, not dead. Tonight. I'll be there."

"I love you," she whispered.

"I love you," I said. I could have whispered it back, but I didn't. I wanted to make sure Kylie heard me.

CHAPTER 7

THEY SAY NEW YORK is the city that never sleeps. But at a quarter to three on a moonlit Tuesday morning in May, the stretch of Central Park West that we were driving on was crapped out like a cat on a porch swing.

Another hour or so, and things would start to stir: the predawn joggers, the early morning sanitation crews, and those age-old, break-of-day stalwarts, the *New York Times* delivery trucks, dropping off bundles of last night's bad tidings to every doorman along this strip of overpriced real estate.

Kylie and I also had some bad news to deliver. Only we couldn't leave it with the doorman and move on. We had to wake up a family in the middle of the night and change their lives forever. It's the suckiest part of our job, and it never gets easier.

Aubrey Davenport's sister, Claudia, and her brother-in-law, Nick Moretti, lived on the eighth floor of a prewar, redbrick building on a tree-lined street between Broadway and West End Avenue.

We had the doorman ring up first. It wouldn't soften the blow for the Morettis, but it gave them a few minutes to brace themselves. By the time Kylie and I got to their door and showed them our badges, they were expecting the worst. We were there to confirm it.

"Is it Aubrey?" Nick Moretti asked.

"Yes, sir," Kylie said. "Her body was found on Roosevelt Island. She was murdered. We are both very sorry for your loss."

Claudia was wearing a lavender robe. Nick had thrown on a pair of jeans and a Jets sweatshirt. She fell into his arms and began sobbing into his chest. Holding her tight, he eased her onto a sofa, and they sat down.

We stood.

It took five minutes before either of them looked up. Finally, Nick asked the inevitable. "Do you know who did it?"

"Not yet, sir," Kylie said. "But we will."

Claudia leaned over and whispered something in her husband's ear.

He shook his head. "Don't go there, Claudia."

"How could I *not* go there?" she said, pulling away and turning to me. "I warned her. Over and over and over. I was the pushy big sister—the voice of doom—but I was right, and now she's dead."

The people who are closest to the victim are the ones who can help us most in the investigation, but usually they are too numb to answer questions immediately, so we try to schedule an interview as soon as they get past the initial shock. But Claudia Moretti seemed to have answers that couldn't wait.

"You warned her about what?" I asked.

"Janek. I said, 'Get a restraining order. Get a gun. He'll kill you.'"

"Tell us about Janek."

"Janek Hoffmann, her cameraman. Her *protégé*. She hired him out of film school. He was a kid—maybe twenty-two—and she was thirty-eight. She said he was talented, but who knows? She was sleeping with him."

"But what made you tell your sister to get a gun?" Kylie asked, trying to get Claudia back on track. "Why did you think Janek was going to kill her?"

"They fought all the time. One minute they'd be like two lovebirds, and the next minute they were like cats and dogs. He was unpredictable. And scary. The man has a terrible temper."

Nick jumped in. "Temper, my ass," he said. "It was straight-up 'roid rage. He was always juiced up. One time they were at a restaurant, and Janek got pissed at the waiter, so he smashed him in the face with one of those oversized pepper mills. Sent the guy to the hospital with a broken jaw."

"Did he ever hit Aubrey?"

"Plenty," Nick said.

"Did she call the police?" Kylie asked.

"Aubrey wasn't the type to do anything like that," Claudia said. "She always needed to solve things her own way, in her own time. She fired him a couple of times, but she always took him back. I could never understand why."

"Jesus, Claudia. Take the blinders off. That muscle-bound dick was always belting her around. She kept coming back for more because that was a turn-on for Aubrey. She was a total sex—"

"Stop! Stop! Stop!" Claudia screamed.

Nick reached out to put his arms around her. "Sweetheart, I'm sorry. I didn't mean to—"

She shoved him aside. "She's dead. Stop judging her!" Claudia shrieked, and ran out of the room in tears.

Nick took a few steps after her, stopped, and then turned to us. "I'll be back," he said. "Don't go."

We didn't move. With or without his invitation, we had no intention of going anywhere.

FOLLOW-UP TO THE *SUNDAY TIMES*
BESTSELLER *NEVER NEVER*

Fifty Fifty

James Patterson
& Candice Fox

**It's not easy being a good detective . . .
when your brother's a serial killer.**

Sam Blue stands accused of the brutal murders of
three young students, their bodies dumped near
the Georges River. Only one person believes he is
innocent: his sister, Detective Harriet Blue. And she's
determined to prove it.

Except she's now been banished to the outback town
of Last Chance Valley (population 75), where a diary
found on the roadside outlines a shocking plan – the
massacre of the entire town. And the first death,
shortly after Harry's arrival, suggests the clock is
already ticking.

Meanwhile, back in Sydney, a young woman holds the
key to crack Sam's case wide open.

**If only she could escape the madman
holding her hostage . . .**

a r r o w b o o k s

Also by James Patterson

ALEX CROSS NOVELS

Along Came a Spider • Kiss the Girls • Jack and Jill •
Cat and Mouse • Pop Goes the Weasel • Roses are Red •
Violets are Blue • Four Blind Mice • The Big Bad Wolf •
London Bridges • Mary, Mary • Cross • Double Cross •
Cross Country • Alex Cross's Trial (*with Richard DiLallo*) •
I, Alex Cross • Cross Fire • Kill Alex Cross • Merry
Christmas, Alex Cross • Alex Cross, Run • Cross My
Heart • Hope to Die • Cross Justice • Cross the Line •
The People vs. Alex Cross

THE WOMEN'S MURDER CLUB SERIES

1st to Die • 2nd Chance (*with Andrew Gross*) • 3rd Degree
(*with Andrew Gross*) • 4th of July (*with Maxine Paetro*) • The 5th
Horseman (*with Maxine Paetro*) • The 6th Target (*with Maxine
Paetro*) • 7th Heaven (*with Maxine Paetro*) • 8th Confession
(*with Maxine Paetro*) • 9th Judgement (*with Maxine Paetro*) •
10th Anniversary (*with Maxine Paetro*) • 11th Hour (*with Maxine
Paetro*) • 12th of Never (*with Maxine Paetro*) • Unlucky 13
(*with Maxine Paetro*) • 14th Deadly Sin (*with Maxine Paetro*) •
15th Affair (*with Maxine Paetro*) • 16th Seduction (*with Maxine
Paetro*) • 17th Suspect (*with Maxine Paetro*)

DETECTIVE MICHAEL BENNETT SERIES

Step on a Crack (*with Michael Ledwidge*) • Run for Your Life
(*with Michael Ledwidge*) • Worst Case (*with Michael Ledwidge*) •
Tick Tock (*with Michael Ledwidge*) • I, Michael Bennett
(*with Michael Ledwidge*) • Gone (*with Michael Ledwidge*) •
Burn (*with Michael Ledwidge*) • Alert (*with Michael Ledwidge*) •
Bullseye (*with Michael Ledwidge*) • Haunted (*with James O. Born*)

PRIVATE NOVELS

Private (*with Maxine Paetro*) • Private London (*with Mark Pearson*) • Private Games (*with Mark Sullivan*) • Private: No. 1 Suspect (*with Maxine Paetro*) • Private Berlin (*with Mark Sullivan*) • Private Down Under (*with Michael White*) • Private L.A. (*with Mark Sullivan*) • Private India (*with Ashwin Sanghi*) • Private Vegas (*with Maxine Paetro*) • Private Sydney (*with Kathryn Fox*) • Private Paris (*with Mark Sullivan*) • The Games (*with Mark Sullivan*) • Private Delhi (*with Ashwin Sanghi*)

NYPD RED SERIES

NYPD Red (*with Marshall Karp*) • NYPD Red 2 (*with Marshall Karp*) • NYPD Red 3 (*with Marshall Karp*) • NYPD Red 4 (*with Marshall Karp*)

DETECTIVE HARRIET BLUE SERIES

Never Never (*with Candice Fox*) • Fifty Fifty (*with Candice Fox*)

STAND-ALONE THRILLERS

The Thomas Berryman Number • Sail (*with Howard Roughan*) • Swimsuit (*with Maxine Paetro*) • Don't Blink (*with Howard Roughan*) • Postcard Killers (*with Liza Marklund*) • Toys (*with Neil McMahon*) • Now You See Her (*with Michael Ledwidge*) • Kill Me If You Can (*with Marshall Karp*) • Guilty Wives (*with David Ellis*) • Zoo (*with Michael Ledwidge*) • Second Honeymoon (*with Howard Roughan*) • Mistress (*with David Ellis*) • Invisible (*with David Ellis*) • Truth or Die (*with Howard Roughan*) • Murder House (*with David Ellis*) • Woman of God (*with Maxine Paetro*) • Hide and Seek • Humans, Bow Down (*with Emily Raymond*) • The Black Book (*with David Ellis*) • Murder Games (*with Howard Roughan*) • Black Market • The Midnight Club • The Store (*with Richard DiLallo*)

NON-FICTION

Torn Apart (*with Hal and Cory Friedman*) • The Murder of
King Tut (*with Martin Dugard*)

ROMANCE

Sundays at Tiffany's (*with Gabrielle Charbonnet*) • The
Christmas Wedding (*with Richard DiLallo*) • First Love (*with
Emily Raymond*) • Two from the Heart (*with Frank Costantini,
Emily Raymond and Brian Sitts*)

OTHER TITLES

Miracle at Augusta (*with Peter de Jonge*) • Penguins of
America (*with Jack Patterson*)

FAMILY OF PAGE-TURNERS

MIDDLE SCHOOL BOOKS

The Worst Years of My Life (*with Chris Tebbetts*) • Get Me
Out of Here! (*with Chris Tebbetts*) • My Brother Is a Big, Fat
Liar (*with Lisa Papademetriou*) • How I Survived Bullies,
Broccoli, and Snake Hill (*with Chris Tebbetts*) • Ultimate
Showdown (*with Julia Bergen*) • Save Rafe! (*with Chris
Tebbetts*) • Just My Rotten Luck (*with Chris Tebbetts*) •
Dog's Best Friend (*with Chris Tebbetts*) •
Escape to Australia (*with Martin Chatterton*)

I FUNNY SERIES

I Funny (*with Chris Grabenstein*) • I Even Funnier (*with Chris
Grabenstein*) • I Totally Funniest (*with Chris Grabenstein*) •
I Funny TV (*with Chris Grabenstein*) • School of
Laughs (*with Chris Grabenstein*)

TREASURE HUNTERS SERIES

Treasure Hunters (*with Chris Grabenstein*) • Danger Down the Nile (*with Chris Grabenstein*) • Secret of the Forbidden City (*with Chris Grabenstein*) • Peril at the Top of the World (*with Chris Grabenstein*) • Quest for the City of Gold (*with Chris Grabenstein*)

HOUSE OF ROBOTS SERIES

House of Robots (*with Chris Grabenstein*) • Robots Go Wild! (*with Chris Grabenstein*) • Robot Revolution (*with Chris Grabenstein*)

JACKY HA-HA SERIES

Jacky Ha-Ha (*with Chris Grabenstein*) • My Life is a Joke (*with Chris Grabenstein*)

OTHER ILLUSTRATED NOVELS

Kenny Wright: Superhero (*with Chris Tebbetts*) • Homeroom Diaries (*with Lisa Papademetriou*) • Word of Mouse (*with Chris Grabenstein*) • Pottymouth and Stoopid (*with Chris Grabenstein*) • Laugh Out Loud (*with Chris Grabenstein*)

MAXIMUM RIDE SERIES

The Angel Experiment • School's Out Forever • Saving the World and Other Extreme Sports • The Final Warning • Max • Fang • Angel • Nevermore • Forever

CONFESSIONS SERIES

Confessions of a Murder Suspect (*with Maxine Paetro*) • The Private School Murders (*with Maxine Paetro*) • The Paris Mysteries (*with Maxine Paetro*) • The Murder of an Angel (*with Maxine Paetro*)

WITCH & WIZARD SERIES

Witch & Wizard (*with Gabrielle Charbonnet*) • The Gift (*with Ned Rust*) • The Fire (*with Jill Dembowski*) • The Kiss (*with Jill Dembowski*) • The Lost (*with Emily Raymond*)

DANIEL X SERIES

The Dangerous Days of Daniel X (*with Michael Ledwidge*) • Watch the Skies (*with Ned Rust*) • Demons and Druids (*with Adam Sadler*) • Game Over (*with Ned Rust*) • Armageddon (*with Chris Grabenstein*) • Lights Out (*with Chris Grabenstein*)

OTHER TITLES

Cradle and All • Crazy House (*with Gabrielle Charbonnet*) • Expelled (*with Emily Raymond*)

GRAPHIC NOVELS

Daniel X: Alien Hunter (*with Leopoldo Gout*) • Maximum Ride: Manga Vols. 1–9 (*with NaRae Lee*)

PICTURE BOOKS

Give Please a Chance (*with Bill O'Reilly*) • Big Words for Little Geniuses (*with Susan Patterson*) • Give Thank You a Try • The Candies Save Christmas

For more information about James Patterson's novels, visit www.jamespatterson.co.uk

Or become a fan on Facebook